COMPUTING MADE SIMPLE

Booksellers and customers agree, this is the best liked and most user friendly series of Computer books for PC users.

The original and the best. These books sell fast!

These books explain the basics of software packages and computer topics in a clear and simple manner, providing just enough information to get started. For users who want an insight into software packages and computers without being overwhelmed by technical terminology they are ideal.

- **Easy to Follow**
- **Task Based**
- **Jargon Free**
- **Easy Steps**
- **Practical**
- **Excellent Value**

ALL YOU NEED TO GET STARTED

BESTSELLER
Works for Windows 3.1 (Version 3)
P. K. McBride
0 7506 2065 X   1994

Lotus 1-2-3 (2.4 DOS Version)
Ian Robertson
0 7506 2066 8   1994

WordPerfect (DOS 6.0)
Stephen Copestake
0 7506 2068 4   1994

BESTSELLER
MS DOS (Up To Version 6.22)
Ian Sinclair
0 7506 2069 2   1994

BESTSELLER
Excel For Windows 3.1 (Version 5)
Stephen Morris
0 7506 2070 6   1994

BESTSELLER
Word For Windows 3.1 (Version 6)
Keith Brindley
0 7506 2071 4   1994

BESTSELLER
Windows 3.1
P. K. McBride
0 7506 2072 2   1994

BESTSELLER
Windows 95
P. K. McBride
0 7506 2306 3   1995

Lotus 1-2-3 for Windows 3.1 (Version 5)
Stephen Morris
0 7506 2307 1   1995

BESTSELLER
Access For Windows 3.1 (Version 2)
Moira Stephen
0 7506 2309 8   1995

BESTSELLER
Internet for Windows 3.1
P. K. McBride
0 7506 2311 X   1995

Pageplus for Windows 3.1 (Version 3)
Ian Sinclair
0 7506 2312 8   1995

Hard Drives
Ian Sinclair
0 7506 2313 6   1995

BESTSELLER
Multimedia for Windows 3.1
Simon Collin
0 7506 2314 4   1995

Powerpoint for Windows 3.1 (Version 4.0)
Moira Stephen
0 7506 2420 5   1995

Office 95
P. K. McBride
0 7506 2625 9   1995

Word Pro for Windows 3.1 (Version 4.0)
Moira Stephen
0 7506 2626 7   1995

BESTSELLER
Word for Windows 95 (Version 7)
Keith Brindley
0 7506 2815 4   1996

BESTSELLER
Excel for Windows 95 (Version 7)
Stephen Morris
0 7506 2816 2   1996

Powerpoint for Windows 95 (Version 7)
Moira Stephen
0 7506 2817 0   1996

BESTSELLER
Access for Windows 95 (Version 7)
Moira Stephen
0 7506 2818 9   1996

BESTSELLER
Internet for Windows 95
P. K. McBride
0 7506 2835 9   1996

Internet Resources
P. K. McBride
0 7506 2836 7   1996

Microsoft Networking
P. K. McBride
0 7506 2837 5   1996

Designing Internet Home Pages
Lilian Hobbs
0 7506 2941 X   1996

BESTSELLER
Works for Windows 95 (Version 4.0)
P. K. McBride
0 7506 3396 4   1996

NEW
Windows NT (Version 4.0)
Lilian Hobbs
0 7506 3511 8   1997

NEW
Compuserve
Keith Brindley
0 7506 3512 6   1997

NEW
Microsoft Internet Explorer
Sam Kennington
0 7506 3513 4   1997

NEW
Netscape Navigator
Sam Kennington
0 7506 3514 2   1997

NEW
Searching The Internet
Sam Kennington
0 7506 3794 3   1997

NEW
The Internet for Windows 3.1 (Second Edition)
P. K. McBride
0 7506 3795 1   1997

NEW
The Internet for Windows 95 (Second Edition)
P. K. McBride
0 7506 3846 X   1997

NEW
Office 97 for Windows
P. K. McBride
0 7506 3798 6   1997

NEW
Powerpoint 97 For Windows
Moira Stephen
0 7506 3799 4   1997

NEW
Access 97 For Windows
Moira Stephen
0 7506 3800 1   1997

NEW
Word 97 For Windows
Keith Brindley
0 7506 3801 X   1997

NEW
Excel 97 For Windows
Stephen Morris
0 7506 3802 8   1997

C

Made Simple

Conor Sexton

MADE SIMPLE
BOOKS

Made Simple
An imprint of Butterworth-Heinemann
Linacre House, Jordan Hill, Oxford OX2 8DP
225 Wildwood Avenue, Woburn, MA 01801-2041
A division of Reed Educational and Professional Publishing Ltd

Ɑ   A member of the Reed Elsevier plc group

OXFORD BOSTON JOHANNESBURG
MELBOURNE NEW DELHI SINGAPORE

First published 1997
Reprinted 1998

TRADEMARKS/REGISTERED TRADEMARKS
Computer hardware and software brand names mentioned in this book are protected
by their respective trademarks and are acknowledged.

British Library Cataloguing in Publication Data
A catalogue record for this book is available from the British Library

ISBN 0 7506 3244 5

Typeset by P.K.McBride, Southampton

Archtype, Bash Casual, Cotswold and Gravity fonts from Advanced Graphics Ltd
Icons designed by Sarah Ward © 1994
Printed and bound in Great Britain by Scotprint, Musselburgh, Scotland

Contents

Preface

C Programming Made Simple is a straightforward presentation of how to write computer programs in the Standard C language. It is deliberately light in tone, avoids as far as possible the more complicated parts of the C language and concentrates on getting aspiring C programmers up to speed in the shortest possible time.

The book should be suitable as an introductory guide for beginning C programmers and for students taking a programming course. Particularly with the latter group in mind, *C Programming Made Simple* presents, in exercise form with answers, more than 30 complete, non-trivial and sometimes even useful programs.

This book covers all the essentials of C but does not deal with the 'dark corners' of the language – for example, how the statement x++ - x++; is evaluated. It is not intended for experienced C programmers other than as a general introductory reference, or for compiler writers at all. For such readers, I recommend my own *Newnes C Pocket Book*, second edition (Butterworth-Heinemann, 1996) and (highly) *C: A Reference Manual* (Prentice Hall, 1995) by Harbison and Steele.

When Butterworth-Heinemann asked me to do *C Programming Made Simple*, I became aware that the main challenge was in producing a text much lighter in weight (both literally and figuratively) than my previous C and C++ books. The priority for a *Made Simple* text is to help the reader to get the most results possible as quickly as possible and for the minimum effort expended. For this book, it means that the first chapter must take a lightning tour through only absolutely essential aspects of the C language, and must absolutely as quickly as possible get the reader to the point of being able to write full programs. The first chapter tries to achieve this ambitious goal.

Chapter 2 shows how C declares and defines data. Chapter 3 takes the 'short path' through the rules for writing C functions while trying not to omit anything vital. Chapters 4 and 5 deal with arithmetic and flow-control aspects of C: how to do sums and how to write branch and loop instructions. Chapter 6 does a combined treatment of arrays and structures, introducing use of pointers with both. Chapter 7 presents somewhat more-advanced information on pointers, while Chapter 8 introduces the C Library, including file handling. Each chapter presents at the end between 3 and 5 practical exercises, for which full answers are given in Chapter 10. Chapter 9 gives a summary of the characteristics of important C Library functions.

I was enthusiastic about writing this book. It is aimed more at the novice than at the expert. I have tried to make its tone correspondingly light and its prose correspondingly simple, while hitting all the important points. I hope you find it useful.

Conor Sexton

November, 1996

1 A quick start with C

Background to the C language

C is to technical computer programming what COBOL is to business software development. While C can be used for all kinds of applications, it is particularly suitable for development of 'techie' software like operating systems, graphical interfaces, communications drivers and database managers. Since it first appeared in 1978, the C programming language has become a language of choice for software developers working in many different application areas. It is now widely used by millions of programmers. Many popular software packages are themselves written in C. Why is C so popular? Here are a few reasons:

- **C is powerful**: it can do all the jobs that high-level languages, like COBOL, can do and it mimics low-level assembler languages. With the high-level stuff, you can do business programming. With the assembler-like bits (no pun intended), you can program devices and registers or write the occasional operating system.

- **C is versatile**: a corollary of its power, this means that, while you could not realistically use COBOL to do low-level graphics programming, you *can* use C to update the creditors' ledger.

- **C is portable**: programs written in it work on computers of all kinds, from the humblest PC to the mightiest mainframe. In fact, it's probably true to say that no self-respecting general-purpose computer today *fails* to support the C language.

- **C is ubiquitous**: billions of lines of C code run on millions of computers. Many computing standards are described in terms of C. Because the language has been internationally standardised, your C program is more likely to 'talk to' everyone else's code than if it were written in Kludgevac 407 assembly language.

- **C is in demand**: as a qualification, knowledge of C is a common denominator in the modern software world: a starting point from which people move on to expertise with the software tools (for example, Microsoft's Visual C++) of particular vendors. It is often a basic requirement expressed by employment advertisements. Once having learnt C, a lesser effort is required to adapt that knowledge to the requirements of particular vendors' systems.

The main identifying characteristic of C is that it specifies, in a manner independent of any particular computer system, how to do efficient, low-level, assembly-like operations. C retains the portability of high-level languages as a result of its independence of any specific type of computer, while its low level operations allow C programs to compete with assembly equivalents.

C was first specified in the early 1970s by two employees of AT&T Bell Laboratories in the U.S.A., Brian Kernighan and Dennis Ritchie. The language immediately attracted adherents and in one move of great importance for the computer industry, the UNIX operating system was rewritten in C. Result: UNIX became inherently portable (it would run on pretty much any computer); UNIX was therefore widely implemented (especially in universities where it was almost free of charge); and a generation of C programmers came into being. With the explosion during the 1980s in the availability and use of PCs, C expanded far beyond its UNIX birthplace, and came to dominate software development for the personal computer also.

With the increasing popularity and use of C, many slightly incompatible definitions of the language came into being. In any case, there had never been a formal definition of the C language; the 1978 book by Kernighan and Ritchie *The C Programming Language* was the accepted, if rather loose, definition.

In 1983, ANSI formed a technical committee, X3J11, on C language and run-time library standardisation. The ANSI C standard — formally referred to as American National Standard X3.159-1989 — was adopted by ANSI in 1989 and superseded in 1990 by the ISO 9899:1990 C standard.

The (technically identical) ANSI and ISO C standards have gained remarkable acceptance and have no real competition; the entire C user community is converging on the single standard. Needless to say, this book covers the C language as specified by these standards. Henceforth, I use the ISO designation in preference to ANSI.

Enough background, propaganda and generalities. Let's get coding!

3

The do-nothing program

It is surprising just how much code it takes in most languages to write a program that does nothing, or almost nothing. The do-nothing COBOL program is about 40 lines. Writing a Windows program that displays a blank window takes about 75 lines of (admittedly C) code.

Happily, using pure C (the subject of this book), you can write a usefulness-free C program called **donowt.c** (that's the name of the file it's stored in) in just one line. Here it is:

```
main(){}
```

Short, isn't it? In fact, this is a complete C program. Every C program must consist of one or more *functions*. The code shown above is a function. The function name is **main**. Every C program must have one (and only one) **main** function. The parentheses, (), enclose the names of *parameters* (if any, none in this simple case) which may be received by the function. The curly braces {} are a *compound statement*: in fact a null compound statement because they do not contain any statements. On execution, the program, as might be expected, does nothing.

A more-strictly-correct variant of the do-nothing program is this:

```
#include <stdio.h>
int main(void){return 0;}
```

Note that the whole program shown is stored in a file called **donowt.c**. The **.c** part is necessary, telling the compiler that the file contains a C program; '**donowt**' is at your discretion.

Similarly, **stdio.h** is a *header file* and is designated as such by the trailing **.h**. This is a *standard header file* that contains useful declarations for compilation and execution of the program that follows.

The **int** preceding **main** specifies that the program returns a value (in this case, zero) to the operating system when it is run.

The **void** *keyword* indicates that the **main** function takes no parameters, of which we shall see more later.

Building and running a C program

The program, in the form shown above, cannot be run on any computer. It must first be converted by *compiler* and *linker* programs into *executable code*. If you're using a PC with a Borland Turbo C++ (C++ is a later language that encompasses C) compiler and linker, you can compile **donowt.c** using this command-line:

tcc donowt.c

This produces an output file called **donowt.exe**, which you can run at the command-line, admiring the spectacular lack of results that ensues. A similar sequence for Borland's (non-Turbo) C++ system is:

bcc donowt.c

For some Microsoft C compilers, you can use 'c-ell':

cl donowt.c

More usually, you use the *integrated development environment* (IDE) provided by the Microsoft Visual C++ package.

If you enjoy the good fortune to be working on a UNIX system, the program is compiled and *loaded* (UNIX-speak for linked) using this command-line:

cc donowt.c

The resulting executable program is in a file called **a.out** (for *assembler output*, believe it or not).

While simple programs may be built (compiled and linked) at the command-line, these days it's more likely that you will use an IDE provided by Microsoft, Borland, IBM or another supplier. The IDE uses a menu-driven interface that is better for managing programs of significant size.

It's not the subject of this book to tell you how to use the IDEs of any software supplier. I assume that the information you now have will enable you to build at least simple C programs, and we move forward now to writing programs that actually do something.

Here's one, called **message.c**:

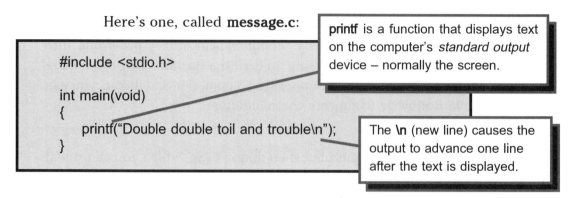

```
#include <stdio.h>

int main(void)
{
    printf("Double double toil and trouble\n");
}
```

printf is a function that displays text on the computer's *standard output* device – normally the screen.

The **\n** (new line) causes the output to advance one line after the text is displayed.

Try entering this program at your computer and building it.

As an exercise, make **message.c** display two lines:

Double double toil and trouble

Fire burn and cauldron bubble

While **message.c** does produce a visible result, it's not very useful. To produce more functional C programs, you must know a minimum set of the basic building-blocks of the C language. Let's turn to those now.

Here is the top-level window shown by Visual C++ running with Microsoft Windows 3.11

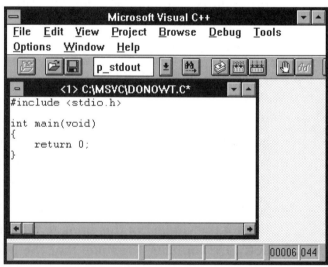

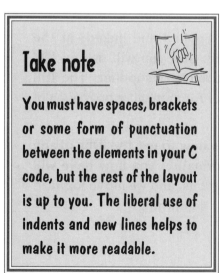

Take note

You must have spaces, brackets or some form of punctuation between the elements in your C code, but the rest of the layout is up to you. The liberal use of indents and new lines helps to make it more readable.

Enough C to get up and running

Data types

To be useful, your C programs must use *variables*. Variables are data objects that may change in value. A variable is given a name by means of a definition, which allocates storage space for the data and associates the storage location with the variable name. The C language defines four fundamental representations (or *types*) of data:

```
char        a character variable
int         an integer (whole number) variable
float       a fractional-number variable
double      a fractional-number variable with more decimal places
```

Here are some examples of how you define variables in C:

```
int         apples;         // to hold whole numbers
char        letter;         // character value e.g.: 'b'
float       balance;        // bank balance
double      pi = 3.14;      // high-precision variable
char        textline[80] = "To be or not to be, that is the question";
```

The first three of these simply set up the storage space. The last two examples also assign values to the variables. After compilation, **apples**, **letter** and **balance** will be there ready to store suitable data, but **pi** will hold 3.14 and **textline** will have its quote from Hamlet.

Statements and expressions

Having defined some variables of various types as part of your program, you will need to combine the variables in *expressions* to make them useful. In a circular definition of the sort beloved of compiler writers, an expression is any valid combination of *function names*, variables, *constants*, *operators* and *subexpressions*. A simple statement is an expression terminated by a semicolon.

The following are all expressions:

```
a = 5
printf("Double double toil and trouble\n")
a = b + c
```

You can assign an expression to a variable:

```
a = printf("Double double toil and trouble\n");
```

In this statement, **a** is assigned the value returned by the function **printf** – the number of characters output by **printf**.

More usefully:

```
a = b + c;
```

assigns to **a** the sum of the values of variables **b** and **c**.

Statements of this kind may optionally be grouped inside pairs of curly braces {}to form a compound statement:

```
{
    printf("Two statements...\n");
    printf("that are logically one\n");
}
```

That a compound statement is a single logical entity is illustrated by the *conditional statement*:

```
    if (s == 2)     // equality check!! NOT the assignment (s = 2)
{
    printf("Two statements...\n");
    printf("that are logically one\n");
}
```

If the variable **s** has the value 2, both **printf**s are executed.

Where the two statements are simple and not compound:

```
if (s == 2)
    printf("Two statements...\n");
printf("that are logically distinct\n");
```

Here only the first statement is conditional on the result of the **if** test. The second **printf** is executed even if **s** is not equal to 2.

Functions

A function is a body of C code called from another part of the program. Every C program is a collection of functions. **main** is a special function: you must specify it in every C program you write. **main** in turn usually calls a number of programmer-defined functions (ones that you have created and named) to do the processing required of the program.

Here is a C program, **twofunc.c**, containing two functions:

```c
/* Two-function program */
#include <stdio.h>
void myfunc(void);    /* 'myfunc' declaration */
int main(void)
{
    printf("When shall we three meet again?\n");
    myfunc();                  // call
    return(0);
}

void myfunc(void)              //definition
{
    printf("In thunder, lightning and in rain\n");
}
/* End of program text */
```

> /* ... */ indicate a comment. The compiler ignores everything within these.

> // also marks a comment. The compiler ignores the rest of the line after //

When it is run, **twofunc.c** displays the lines of text on screen:

    When shall we three meet again?
    In thunder, lightning and in rain

The statement

    myfunc();

is the call from **main** to the function **myfunc**.

The various parts of a C function are critical to your understanding of the C language and to your ability to program in it. You should take the time here to understand how a function is declared, called and defined; it will save you a lot of confusion later. The function **myfunc** (as all functions should be) is expressed in three parts:

The *declaration* (also called a function *prototype*):

    void myfunc(void);

which announces to the compiler the existence of **myfunc**.

The *call*:

    myfunc();

which executes the function's code.

The *definition* of the function itself:

```
void myfunc(void)
{
    printf("In thunder, lightning and in rain\n");
}
```

Data input

Statements and functions together allow you to write powerful C programs. But you need one more thing: the ability to input from and output to external devices such as files, screen displays and printers. The *standard library* contains many functions that perform input/output (I/O); **getchar** gets a character from the keyboard:

```
int c;
c = getchar();
```

When **getchar** executes, the program stops, waiting for you to enter a character followed by [**Enter**]. After you make the entry, **c** contains that character, but not [**Enter**].

Here are three library functions that carry out operations on character strings stored in arrays:

```
gets(<char array>);     // Read a string into an array
atoi(<char array>);     // Convert text to integer
atof(<char array>);     // Convert text to fraction
```

Using the following definitions:

```
char        instring[20];
int         binval;
double      floatval;
```

the statement

```
gets(instring);
```

reads from the standard input device a string of maximum length 20 characters. There is nothing to stop the entry of data greater than 20 characters long; if there are more than 20 characters, the end of the array is overrun. The character contents of *instring* (say "598") may then be converted to their numeric equivalent value (a number slightly less than 600) using the library function **atoi**:

```
binval = atoi(instring);
```

You can convert the contents of *instring* (say "1.2345") into their fractional numeric equivalent value (a number slightly less than $1^1/_4$) using the library function **atof**:

```
floatval = atof(instring);
```

The C preprocessor

To make your C program executable, you must build it using the techniques described on page 5. As part of this build procedure you (most likely unwittingly) call the *C preprocessor*. The preprocessor carries out necessary text substitutions on the source code and causes inclusion of optional header files into the source code.

You have already seen inclusion of the header file **stdio.h**. When the preprocessor encounters the line:

```
#include <stdio.h>
```

it expands within the text of your program the contents of the file **stdio.h**. These contents include, among other things, declarations (prototypes) of library functions such as **printf**. Similarly, the standard header file **stdlib.h** contains declarations for the library functions **atoi** and **atof** referred to above, and should be **#include**d where those functions are used.

You can create and include your own header files, idenitifed by **.h**:

```
#include "myheader.h"
```

See page 42 for the significance of <angle brackets> and "quotes".

If your program contains the line:

```
#define MAX 50
```

the preprocessor again recognises the leading **#** character and substitutes all occurrences in the program of the text pattern **MAX** with the pattern 50.

When the preprocessor has handled all **#include**, **#define** and other preprocessor *directives*, the changed source code is then passed to the compiler.

Your first real C program

You now know enough about C (just!) to understand a non-trivial program and to get it working.

As its name suggests, the program **nameaddr.c** takes as input and displays your name and address. The name and address data are stored as character arrays and a total of three functions read and display the data using library functions.

Name and address

```c
/*****************************************************************
 *
 *      'nameaddr.c' — Program to accept input of and
 *              display the user's name and address
 *
 *****************************************************************/
#include <stdio.h>

void getdata(char *, char *, char *, char *);
void dispdata(char *, char *, char *, char *);

int main(void)
{
    //      Define variables to hold name and address data
    char name[20];
    char addr1[30], addr2[30], addr3[30];

    //      Call function to accept keyboard input
    getdata(name, addr1, addr2, addr3);

    //      Call function to display the user-input data
    dispdata(name, addr1, addr2, addr3);

    //      Finished, stop program
    return(0);
}
```

> The comma is a separator. Here it separates the four arguments passed to **getdata**.

```
void getdata(char *n, char *a1, char *a2, char *a3)
{
    printf("Enter name: ");
    gets(n);
    printf("Enter address 1: ");
    gets(a1);
    printf("Enter address 2: ");
    gets(a2);
    printf("Enter address 3: ");
    gets(a3);
}

void dispdata(char *name, char *addr1, char *addr2, char *addr3)
{
    printf("\nName and address details:\n\n");
    printf("\t%s\n", name);
    printf("\t%s\n", addr1);
    printf("\t%s\n", addr2);
    printf("\t%s\n", addr3);
}
```

As it must at this stage of your learning-curve on the path to being an expert C programmer, **nameaddr.c** introduces some C syntax that you haven't encountered yet. But you do know enough to assimilate the program as a whole and, in so doing, to extend your knowledge of C further.

The most striking aspect of **nameaddr.c** compared to all the code that you have seen up to now is that two of the functions take *parameters*. Both **getdata** and **dispdata** take four character-array parameters. In the call to **dispdata**:

```
//    Call function to display the user-input data
dispdata(name, addr1, addr2, addr3);
```

the contents of the four named character arrays are made available to the code of the function, seen later in the program. That code contains the *function header*:

```
void dispdata(char *name, char *addr1, char *addr2, char *addr3)
```

Here **name**, **addr1**, **addr2** and **addr3** become, in effect, copies of the four arrays 'sent' as part of the function call. **dispdata** then displays the contents of these four arrays. The notation **char *** means *character pointer* and is explained later in this chapter and in the rest of the book. For now, it is enough for you to know that each of the four character pointers **name**, **addr1**, **addr2** and **addr3** acts as a 'handle' on the original data 'sent' by the function call. Trust me!

In the opposite sense to **dispdata**, **getdata** takes four parameters – empty arrays in this case – and fills them up with name and address data using some of the library functions described earlier.

After that, it's details. The only other significant extra notation is in the **printf** statements that are part of **dispdata**:

```
printf("\nName and address details:\n\n");
printf("\t%s\n", name);
```

Each newline (**\n**) character is output to the screen as a line-shift-up. When **printf** sends the vertical tab character **\t** to the screen, the effect is indentation, usually of about eight characters. Lastly, the **%s** specification is a *format code* which tells **printf** that the variable after the *format string* is a *character string*. See opposite for more on **printf**.

When you build the program, you should run **nameaddr.exe** (**a.out** if you're using UNIX) at the command-line. Prompts appear for each of the pieces of data in turn. At the end, all the data you entered is displayed. Text that I entered as the program user is shown in bold:

```
Enter name: Conor Sexton
Enter address 1: Butterworth-Heinemann
Enter address 2: Oxford OX2 8DP
Enter address 3: UK
Name and address details:
    Conor Sexton
    Butterworth-Heinemann
    Oxford OX2 8DP
    UK
```

Now. That wasn't too hard, was it? You're already well past the starting mark on our journey through C. Stick with me and the rest of the trip won't seem all that long.

Things you need to know

We are going at warp speed through the essential constructs of the C language. So far, I've simply not dealt with a number of important aspects of C. The focus is on rushing you along the short path to minimal competency in C programming. Then, you will be more ready to face the other 90% of the language. Many of the constructs you will have to understand are included in this section.

Standard device I/O

The concept of *standard device* is important in C. If you are using a terminal, you may think of the *standard input* as being the keyboard and the *standard output* as the screen. As you have seen, a C program may read text from the standard input using the **getchar** library function and send text to the standard output using **printf**.

printf is the name of a library function. Its declaration is stored in the header file **stdio.h** and included in C programs by means of the **#include** preprocessor directive (see page 11):

    #include <stdio.h>

stdio.h contains many declarations of library functions, such as **printf**, as well as other useful definitions, including those for **NULL** (pointer to no object, represented as zero) and **EOF** (end-of-file, usually represented as –1).

The **printf** function call includes at least one *argument*. The first argument is always a string and is the format string, delimited by double quotes. ('argument' means much the same thing as 'parameter', the contents of an argument being copied in a function call to the parameter used in the called function's header).

The format string contains two kinds of objects: *ordinary characters*, which are copied to the standard output device, and *format codes*, which are prefixed by a **%**. The format string causes **printf** to output any following arguments in the manner specified by the format codes.

If they are specified, the second and subsequent arguments to **printf** are variables or expressions. You can see this in the next example program.

```
    int main(void)
    {
        int    num = 6;
        float  e = 2.718282;

        printf("Number is %d, fraction is %f\n", num,e);

        return(0);
    }
```

The **printf** call gives this display on the standard output device (screen):

Number is 6, fraction is 2.718282

Fundamental printf format codes are:

%d	decimal integer
%f	floating-point number
%g	double floating-point number
%s	string
%c	character

As you saw in the program **nameaddr.c**, **gets** is a library function that reads character strings from the standard input. **getchar** is a less-powerful variant that reads single characters. The rest of this book presents many more Standard I/O functions.

Branching

You can use the **if** statement to allow decisions and consequent changes in the flow of control to be made by the program logic. Here is a simple example of an **if** statement, where a single statement is subject to the test:

```
    if (nobufs < MAXBUF)              // '<' means 'less than'
        nobufs = nobufs + 1;
```

The variable **nobufs** is only incremented by 1 if its value is initially less than **MAXBUF**.

Two or more statements may be made subject to an **if** by use of a compound statement:

16

```
if (day == 1)
{
    printf("Monday\n");
    week = week + 1;
}
if (day == 2)
{
    printf("Tuesday\n");
    run_sales_report();
}
```

There is an optional **else** clause that can be used where alternative code is to be executed if the test fails. Use **else** where the program logic suggests it:

```
if (day == 1)
{
    printf("Monday\n");
    week = week + 1;
}
else if (day == 2)
    {
        printf("Tuesday\n");
        run_sales_report();
    }
```

Use of **else** here stops execution of the *Tuesday* code if the value of **day** is 1.

Looping

Where the **if** statement allows a branch in the program flow of control, you can use the **for** and **while** statements to allow repeated execution of code in loops.

First, we see the **while** loop:

```
#include <stdio.h>
int main(void)
{
    int x;

    x = 1;
```

17

```
            while (x < 100)
            {
                printf("Number %d\n",x);
                x = x + 1;
            }
            return(0);
        }
```

This program displays all the numbers from 1 to 99 inclusive. Next we have the equivalent **for**-loop construct:

```
        #include <stdio.h>
                            Start  condition
        int main(void)              Loop as long as this is true
        {
            int x;                      Perform this each time round

            for (x = 1; x < 100; x = x + 1)
                printf("Number %d\n",x);

            return(0);
        }
```

The first time into the **for** loop, **x** is set to 1 and checked for being less than 100. On the second and subsequent iterations, **x** is incremented by 1 and checked for being less than 100. When **x** becomes equal to 100, execution of the loop stops. The last number displayed is 99.

There is a third loop form in C, the '**do-while**' construct. You will see this in Chapter 5.

Types for grouping data

C provides two constructs for grouping data of the basic types (**char**, **int** and so on). These are the array and the structure. Whenever you see square brackets [], you know you're dealing with an array. Presence of the **struct** keyword tells you that you are using a structure. Arrays and structures are collectively referred to as *aggregate data types*.

An array consists of one or more data elements all of the same type. Structures consist of members of possibly different types. Any data object may be stored in an array.

You can define array of ten integer variables like this:

    int num[10];

The value within the square brackets [ ], is known as a *subscript*. In the case above, ten adjacent memory locations for integer values are allocated by the compiler. The subscript range is from 0 to 9. When using a variable as a subscript, take care to count from 0 and stop one short of the subscript value. Here is a simple example of use of arrays:

```
/*
 *  Fill integer array with zeros, fill character array with blanks
 */

#include <stdio.h>

int main(void)
{
    int  n[20];
    char    c[20];
    int  i;

    for (i = 0; i < 20; i = i + 1)
    {
        n[i] = 0;
        c[i] = ' ';
    }

    return(0);
}
```

You can see that i starts the iteration with value zero and finishes at 19. If it were incremented to 20, a memory location outside the bounds of the array would be accessed.

Here is an example of a *structure* declaration:

```
    struct rec
    {
        char name[20];
        char addr[50];
        int age;
    };
```

You can see that not all the members of the structure **rec** are of the same type. To define a copy of **struct rec** in memory, you need to make this definition:

```
struct rec person;
```

Now you can assign values to the structure's members using, in two cases, the **strcpy** (string copy) library function:

```
strcpy(person.name, "Will Shakespeare");
strcpy(person.addr, "Stratford on Avon");
person.age = 52;                            // age when he died
```

Inimitable C: pointers

A pointer is the address of a data object in memory. More than any other construct, pointers set C apart from all other languages. PL/1 and Pascal have pointers in their syntax, but these are not as flexible in use as C pointers. You can use pointers everywhere in C code.

A variable definition allocates space for the data and associates a name with that data. The data name refers directly to the data stored at the memory location. Pointers, on the other hand, are data objects that point to other data objects.

You can define a character variable and a character pointer like this:

```
char c;
```
```
char *cptr;
```

cptr is a *pointer to* a data object of type **char**.

The statement:

```
cptr = &c;
```

uses the *address-of* operator (&) to assign the address of **c** to the character pointer **cptr**. After the assignment, **cptr** points to **c**, ***cptr** is the *contents* of or the *object at* the pointer **cptr** and ***cptr** equals **c**.

You can use pointers with data objects of all types, including arrays and pointers themselves. Pointers are particularly powerful in use with arrays. In this introduction, we have only seen simple character pointers. Chapters 6 and 7 go into pointers in rather more detail.

The C Library

C does not have any built-in functions of the type familiar in Pascal and other languages. Functions that provide these features are defined separately in the *C Standard Library*. The functions are stored in the Library in their compiled form. They are linked with your program during the build process. The function **printf** is a familiar example of a library function.

Functions and *macros* used in the C libraries are declared in standard header files. You should use preprocessor directives to include required header files in the source code of any program that uses C library functions. In the case of **printf**, you should include the standard I/O header file **stdio.h**. This is the most important of the standard header files and declares most of the library functions that you will need.

The other standard header files most commonly used are:

stdio.h	standard I-O
string.h	string functions
ctype.h	character class tests
math.h	mathematical functions
stdlib.h	other standard functions

For example, if you use in your program the **strcpy** library function shown earlier, you should first include the **string.h** standard header file:

```
#include <string.h>
```

Your documentation and the Help system supplied with your C compiler will give further information about the available C Library functions and the header files that you need to declare them. You'll also find a lot more information in Chapter 8 of this book.

You're now finished your warp-speed tour of C. Yes, you have seen (well, skimmed really) every major aspect of the C language. The rest, as they say, is details.

Exercises

1. What are the three parts of every properly-written C function? Write any program that inplements all three.

2. Design and implement a structure (a C **struct** declaration) to hold data about car parts and prices. There should be at least three structure members: part number, part name and the part's price. Write a program that uses the structure. Prompt the user to input part data, then display that data.

3. What is wrong with:

   ```
   if (s = 2)
   {
         printf("Two statements...\n");
         printf("that are logically one\n");
   }
   ```

   Why? What happens when the code executes?

4. Write a program containing a **for** loop that displays on the standard output every second number (1, 3, 5....) between 1 and 100, inclusive of both.

5. Write a program that defines and assigns a value to an integer variable, defines a variable of type *pointer-to-int*, assigns the address of the integer to the pointer and displays the integer pointed to.

2 How C handles data

Basic data types and qualifiers

C's data types

To be able to use the power of C effectively in your programs, you need to know more about the ways in which the language represents data. As you saw in Chapter 1, there are four simple data types in C, which are used as *type specifiers* in the definition of variables:

char	a single byte, storing one character
int	an integer of a size dependent on the host computer
float	a single-precision floating-point (real) number
double	a double-precision floating-point (real) number

You can qualify the simple data types with these keywords:

signed   unsigned   long   short   const   volatile

On computers for which the 8-bit byte is the smallest addressable memory space, and therefore the basic data object, the **char** type specifies a variable of one byte in length. **char** specifies enough memory to store any member of the local system's *character set*.

Depending on whether you are using a system with 16-bit, 32-bit or 64-bit addressing and integer size, the sizes of **int**, **float** and **double** data objects vary. Broadly, you can assume that the sizes of addresses and integers using the DOS/Windows 3.X combination is 16 bits; for almost all other systems, they are 32 bits; and for a few, such as the Digital Equipment Corp. Alpha AXP, the sizes are 64 bits. On a majority decision, then, our discussion of type sizes is biased toward the assumption of a 32-bit integer size, with a nod to the 16-bit DOS/Windows convention.

On a computer with a 32-bit processor and the Windows NT, Windows 95, OS/2 or UNIX operating system, the default integer size is 32 bits. An **int** in a C program on such a system is 32 bits (4 bytes). A **float** is also usually implemented in 32 bits, while a **double** takes up 64 bits or eight bytes.

You can combine the basic types with the qualifiers listed above to yield types of sizes varying from the defaults. The table below gives possibilities for combination of the basic data types and the qualifiers.

Type Qualifier	char	int	float	double
signed	X	X		
unsigned	X	X		
short		X		
long		X		X
const	X	X	X	X
volatile	X	X	X	X

The default integer type is signed **int**. If the leftmost bit in the (probably 32-bit) integer bit-pattern is 1, the number is treated as negative; 0 indicates positive. The types **int** and **signed int** are synonymous. **unsigned int** forces the integer value to be positive. The sign-bit is not used and it is possible to accommodate in an unsigned int a positive value twice as large as for an ordinary **int**.

If the size of an **int** is 16 bits, **short int** is generally also 16 bits while **long int** is 32 bits. If the **int** size is 32 bits, **short int** is generally 16 bits and **long int** is also 32 bits.

You can simplify **short int** to just **short**, **unsigned int** to **unsigned** and **long int** to **long**.

The qualifier **const** may be prefixed to any declaration, and specifies that the value to which the data object is initialised cannot be changed.

As well as the possibilities in the table, **signed short int** and **unsigned short int** are legal, as are **signed long int** and **unsigned long int**.

Here are some example declarations that assume a system with a natural 32-bit integer:

```
short x;              // x is 16 bits long and can hold integer values
                      // in the range -32767 and 32767
int y;                // y is 32 bits long and holds integer values
                      // in the range -2147483647 to 2147483647
long z;               // same as 'int' above
unsigned short a;     // sign-bit disabled, can hold positive integer
                      // values up to 65535
```

unsigned b;	// 'int' definition with sign-bit disabled, can hold // positive integer values up to 4294967295

float c;	// c is 32 bits long and can hold a fractional number
	// in a floating-point form in the range
	// 3.403 X 10^38 to 1.175 X 10^-38

double d;	// d is 64 bits long and can hold a fractional number // in the range 1.798 X 10^308 to 2.225 X 10^-308

Here is a program, **maxint.c**, which finds the largest possible numeric value that can be stored in an **int** on your computer:

```
/**************************************************************************
 *
 *      'maxint.c' —   Program to find the largest number that can
 *                     be stored in an 'int' on this computer
 *
 **************************************************************************/
#include <stdio.h>

int main(void)
{
    int shift = 1, accum = 0;

    // loop until a further shift would set the sign bit

    while(shift > 0)
    {
        //  add shift to the accumulator and double it
        accum = accum + shift;
        shift = shift * 2;
    }
    printf("Maximum int value is %d\n", accum);
    return(0);
}
```

This is, if I may say so myself, a rather clever way of solving the problem. The obvious but crude way is to start at 1 and keep adding 1 until the sign-bit changes and the integer goes negative. But on a 32-bit system, this takes somewhat more than two billion additions which, assuming one million per second, will take over half an hour. Run the program to find the maximum integer size on your system.

26

The program does a 'shift and multiply' 32 times and finds the answer through a logarithmic sequence – literally millions of times faster than by repeated addition. When you run the program, its output is:

    Maximum int value is 32767

You should be able to guess from this that I ran the program on a 16-bit system (DOS and Windows 3.11). Had the program run under, say, Windows 95, the maximum value would have been 2147483647.

Initialisation and assignment

When you define a variable in a C program, you should assume that it will initially be set to a garbage value. You should therefore initialise variables, where necessary, when you define them.

In **maxint.c**, **shift** and **accum** are initialised as part of their definition:

    int shift = 1, accum = 0;

Initialisation means that a variable is set to a value at the point of definition; *assignment* separates the setting of value from the definition:

    int shift;
    shift = 1;

You can initialise a variable of type **long int** like this:

    long big_num = 1000000L;

The trailing **L** tells the compiler that the 1000000 is to be a **long** integer.

char variables can be initialised to a character (or numeric) value:

    char c = 'a';
    char d = 97;   // same thing: 97 is ASCII 'a'

Type conversion and casting

In an ideal world, you would ensure that all variables used in a given expression were of the same type. Then no conversions would be needed, for example between integer and fractional, or between character and integer, quantities. But, life isn't that simple. Sometimes, to keep things correct, we must explicitly force conversions between data types. This operation in C is referred to as *type casting*.

Type casting is done using the *unary typecast operator*, which is a type specifier, enclosed in parentheses and prefixed to an expression. The cast does not change the value of the expression but may be used to avoid the consequences of unintended type conversions.

Type conversion can be vital. Imagine you're calculating the total number of days that have elapsed since January 1, 1900. The computation would be something like this:

    days_total = (long)yy * 365 + no_leaps + days_year + dd;

On a 16-bit integer system, the intermediate calculation **yy * 365** exceeds the 32,767 integer size limit if the date is later than September 18, 1989. The intermediate calculation **(long)yy * 365**, forcing **yy** temporarily to be long, works on all systems, having a capacity of 2,147,483,647 in both 16- and 32-bit environments.

In C, the expression 5/7 gives zero, as a result of integer division. If you didn't want this, you could use the typecast operation:

    (float)5/(float)7

to get the fractional result, .71428...

Expression type

Every expression has a type. If the expression contains an assignment, its type will be that of the variable being assigned to; if not, the expression will be of a type determined by its constituent parts.

For example, given the definitions:

    int a;
    double b, c, d;

the expression:

    a = b * c / d

is of type **int**, while **b * c / d** on its own is of type **double**. Since **double** is a 'larger' type than **int**, information may be lost here across the assignment. It's up to you, the programmer, to ensure that this does not happen. In practice, the best way you can do this is to make sure that the variable being assigned to has enough capacity to take the assignment.

Naming conventions

Variables are defined or declared by association of a type specifier and variable name. For simple data objects, declarations and definitions are usually the same; it is enough for now to say that all definitions are declarations but that the converse is not true.

There are in C some simple rules concerning the names that may be used for variables. These names are also called *identifiers*.

A variable name should not be a library function name (see Chapter 9) and must not be one of these keywords (*reserved words*):

auto	break	case	char	const
continue	default	do	double	else
enum	extern	float	for	goto
if	int	long	register	return
short	signed	sizeof	static	struct
switch	typedef	union	unsigned	void
volatile	while			

A variable name is a sequence of letters and digits. Distinction is made between upper and lower case letters. The underscore _ also counts as a character and should be used for clarity in variable names:

    next_record_from_file

being more readable than **nextrecordfromfile**. With the rise of GUI development environments, the following convention has also become acceptable and good practice:

    nextRecordFromFile

Don't use punctuation, control and other special characters in variable names. Also, don't use the underscore at the start of variable names; if you do, there may be a clash with the names of certain library functions. Variable names may be any length, but the C compiler may treat only the first 31 characters as significant.

Here are some examples of incorrect variable name definitions:

    int bank-bal   // Wrong! incorrect hyphen
    int 1sttime   // Wrong! leading number
    int new?acc   // Wrong! invalid character

Arithmetic operations

You can perform calculations with these arithmetic operators:

+ addition
- subtraction
* multiplication
/ division
% modulus

Use of the division operator, /, with two or more integer operands causes integer division and consequent truncation:

3/5 equals zero

5/3 equals 1

The *modulus* or 'remainder' operator, **%**, may only be used with *operands* of type **int** or **char**. You can't use it with **float** or **double** operands. Multiplication, division and modulus operations are done before addition and subtraction. *Unary minus* operations (for example, **-(a + b)**, as opposed to the binary **a - b**) are carried out before any of these. You can see the *precedence* of the arithmetic operators from this series of assignments:

```
int  x = 5;
int  y = 6;
int  z = 7;
int  result;
     ...
result = x + y * z;      // result == 47
result = y / x * z;      // result == 7
result = (x + y) * z;    // result == 77
result = -y * z + x;     // result == -37
result = z / x % y;      // result == 1
```

You may have noticed that there is no operator for exponentiation: you have no way of expressing something like *x to the power 5*. To do this, you must use the **pow** library function described in Chapter 9.

Here is an program, called **sum1ton.c**, that implements the so-called Abelian series after the famous mathematician Abel. As a bright 10-year-old, young Abel and his class at school were set time-killing exercises by their teacher. One such was the job of adding all the numbers from 1 to 100. Abel, using his series, was able instantly to present the result to his teacher. The series is described by the equation $t = n(n + 1)/2$, where **t** is the total and **n** is the number at the end of the series.

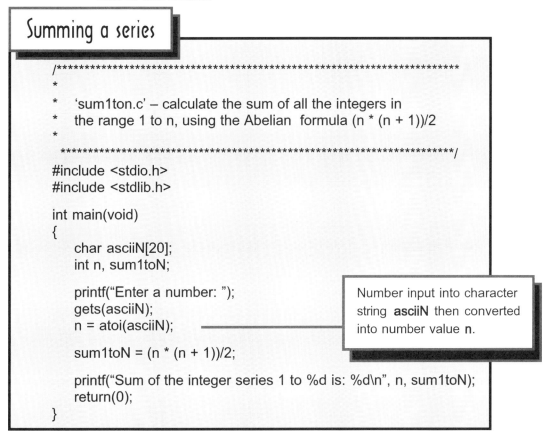

Summing a series

```
/************************************************************************
*
*   'sum1ton.c' – calculate the sum of all the integers in
*   the range 1 to n, using the Abelian formula (n * (n + 1))/2
*
************************************************************************/
#include <stdio.h>
#include <stdlib.h>

int main(void)
{
    char asciiN[20];
    int n, sum1toN;

    printf("Enter a number: ");
    gets(asciiN);
    n = atoi(asciiN);

    sum1toN = (n * (n + 1))/2;

    printf("Sum of the integer series 1 to %d is: %d\n", n, sum1toN);
    return(0);
}
```

Number input into character string **asciiN** then converted into number value **n**.

Try entering and building this program.

When you run it, you are prompted to enter the limit of the series to be summed. The **gets** function reads your answer from the keyboard into the string **asciiN**. The separate characters of the number you entered ('1', '0' and '0' of the number 100) are collectively converted to the numeric form by the library function **atoi** and are stored in **n**. Abel's formula calculates the sum, which is displayed by the **printf** statement. Here's the expected display (input in bold):

Enter a number: **100**

Sum of the integer series 1 to 100 is: 5050

Different kinds of constants

Every basic data object – **char**, **int**, **float**, **double** – is a number. A number used explicitly, not as the value of a variable, is a *constant*. Constants are such things as the integer 14, the character 'a' and the newline '\n'.

The kinds of constants that you can use in C expressions include:

Integer constants

The integer constant 14 is a data object inherently of type **int**. An integer constant such as 5000000, that on a 16-bit system is too large to be accommodated by an **int** is treated by the compiler as a **long int**.

An integer constant can be prefixed with a leading zero: 014 is interpreted as being of base 8 (*octal*) and equals decimal 12. An integer constant can have the prefix 0x or 0X:

    0x14 or 0X14
    0x2F or 0X2F

The compiler treats these constants as *hexadecimal* (base 16). Hexadecimal 0x14 equals decimal 20. 0x2F equals decimal 47.

Character constants

A character constant is a single character, written in single quotes: 'a'. A character constant is a number. After the definition and initialisation:

    char ch = 'a';

ch contains the numeric value decimal 97. Decimal 97 is the numeric representation of 'a' in the ASCII character set, which is used in many micro- and mini-computers. If a different character set is used, for example EBCDIC, the underlying numeric value of 'a' is different.

For example: '0' (*character zero*) is a character constant with ASCII value 48. '0' is not the same as *numeric zero*, so after the definitions:

    int   n = 0;
    char   c = '0';

the integer **n** contains the value 0; the character **c** contains the value 48.

String constants

You specify character constants with single quotes; *literal string constants* by contrast use double quotes:

"This is a string constant"

A string constant is also known as a *string literal*. The double quotes are not part of the string literal; they only delimit the string.

Floating-point constants

Floating-point constants are always shown as fractional and can be represented in either normal or *scientific notation*:

1.0
335.7692
-.00009
31.415927e-1

Floating point constants are of type **double** unless explicitly suffixed with f or F, as in:

1.7320508F

which is of type **float**.

Special character constants

The newline character '\n' is a character constant. There is a range of these special character constants – also known as *escape sequences*. They are listed on the next page.

Special character constants

```
\n      // newline
\r      // carriage-return
\t      // tab
\f      // formfeed
\b      // backspace
\v      // vertical tab
\a      // audible alarm - BEL
\\      // 'escape' backslash
\?      // 'escape' question-mark
\'      // 'escape' single quote
\"      // 'escape' double quote.
```

The escape sequences are used in place of the less-intuitive code-table numeric values. In **printf** statements, '\n' is commonly used at the end of the format string to denote advance to a new line on the standard output device. You could instead use the equivalent ASCII (octal) numeric code '\012' but this is less intuitively clear, as well as not being portable to systems using code tables other than ASCII.

Other characters can also be *escaped out*. Use of the lone backslash causes any special meaning of the following character to be suppressed. The following character is treated as its literal self. For example, the statement

    printf("This is a double quote symbol: \"\n");

causes this display on the standard output:

    This is a double quote symbol: "

with subsequent advance to a new line, due to the inclusion of "\n".

There are many other special characters which do not have an identifying letter and are represented by their number in the character set, delimited by single quotes. These are examples from the ASCII character set:

    #define   SYN   '\026' // synchronize

    #define   ESC   '\033' // escape

This is a good use of the preprocessor, equating symbolic constants with numeric control characters. The symbolic constant ESC in the middle of a communications program makes more sense than '\033'.

Here is a program, **charform.c**, that shows how the contents of a **char** variable can be interpreted differently using **printf** format codes.

```
/*********************************************************************
 *
 *      'charform.c' — Program to show interpretation of a
 *    character's value according to various
 *    'printf' format codes
 *
 *********************************************************************/
#include <stdio.h>

int main(void)
{
    int c;

    printf("Enter a character: ");
    c = getchar();

    printf("Character %c, Number %d, Hex, %x, Octal %o\n",
                    c, c, c, c);

    return(0);
}
```

The most important purpose of this program is to confirm that a character is no more than a number and that it can be interpreted as different kinds of numbers. Try running it yourself to confirm this. Here's what the display should look like. The character that I input for interpretation was the question-mark.

```
Enter a character: ?
Character ?, Number 63, Hex, 3f, Octal 77
```

Pointers

Pointers and addresses

You have already briefly seen in Chapter 1 how a character pointer is defined and used. The purpose of pointers is to allow the programmer to use variables indirectly, by means of their *memory addresses.*

A pointer contains an address: no memory is allocated for it by the compiler other than the memory required to store that address. It is always an error to use a pointer which has not been initialised to the address of a data object to which memory has been allocated.

The simplest type of pointer, the character pointer, is defined and initialised like this:

```
char    c = 'q';
char    *cp = &c;
```

cp is a **char** pointer, pointing to **c**. The *contents of* or *object at* the variable **c** is later *dereferenced* with ***cp**.

Similarly, you can define and use an *integer pointer* (a pointer that should be used only with variables of type **int**).

```
int i = 6;
int *ip = &i;
```

Taking the example of the integer pointer, you can reflect on the following truisms:

```
i == 6
ip == the address of the integer i
*ip == the object at the address, 6
```

A major confusion arises from the dual use of the ***ip** sequence. The definition of the pointer:

```
int *ip = &i;
```

specifies that the variable **ip** is of type **int ***, or integer pointer. On the other hand, when the pointer is later used and dereferenced:

```
*ip
```

the object at the pointer **ip** (6) is retrieved. If you keep in mind the difference between the sequence ***ip** used when the pointer is being defined and ***ip** used to retrieve the value stored at the pointer, you will move a long way toward being fluent in the use of C pointers.

Pointers to data objects

You can use pointers with all data objects that may be defined in C, including arrays, structures and other pointers. In this section, we're particularly interested in arrays, especially character arrays.

In the definition of the integer pointer above, the address-of operator **&** is used in the initialisation of the pointer **ip** with the address of the integer **i**:

```
int i = 6;
int *ip = &i;
```

The address-of operator must be used when initialising pointers – except when the address of an array is being assigned to a pointer of the same type as the array. In the sequence:

```
char instring[50];
char *cptr = &instring;
```

cptr is in fact initialised to the *address of the address* of the pointer. *An array name is the array's address*; to initialise the pointer with the array's address

```
char *cptr = instring;
```

is all that is needed to do the job correctly. One of the quirks of the C language that causes most inconvenience even for experienced programmers, is the fact that an array's name is its address while the name of any other variable is not.

Next, we define and initialise a character array and set a pointer pointing to the start of the array:

```
char textline[50] = "Many a time and oft on the Rialto";
char *cp = textline;
```

The value of **textline[0]** is the letter 'M'; the value of **textline[1]** is 'a' and so on. Similarly, the value of ***cp** after the pointer has been initialised is 'M'. The value of ***(cp+1)** is 'a' and the value of ***(cp+2)** is 'n'. You will see much more in Chapter 6 of pointers used with arrays.

Here is an example program, **litptr.c**, that uses pointers to traverse a character array one character at a time, displaying each character on the way.

```
/***********************************************************************
 *
 *      'litptr.c' —   Program to display each character in a literal
 *                      string using a simple character pointer
 *
 ***********************************************************************/
#include <stdio.h>

int main(void)
{
    char litstr[50] = "The quality of mercy is not strained";
    char *start, *p;

    start = p = litstr;

    while(*p != '\0')
    {
        printf("%c", *p);
        p++;
    }
    printf("\nString is %d chars long\n", p-start);
    return(0);
}
```

Apart from wondering who said "The quality of mercy..." and in what Shakespeare play, you can examine the pointer technique shown by the program. Both the pointers **start** and **p** are set pointing to the start of the array **litstr**. Then, while the contents of **p** are not the null character, all the individual characters in the array are displayed individually, along with the length of the string:

The quality of mercy is not strained

String is 36 chars long

Notice that the **%c** (character) **printf** format code is used to specify that ***p**, as the object at the pointer, is an individual character within the array. When the length of the string is reported, **%d** is used to display **p-start**, the displacement of **p** from the start of the array **litstr**.

In case you think that this stuff with pointers might only be used by nerds and code-freaks, be disabused of the notion now. Text processing, and other use of pointers, is central to C programming. To be a good C programmer, you have to be good at pointers. On that consoling note, be happy that you have now surmounted one of the steeper obstacles presented by the C language.

Take note

All strings in C are character arrays terminated with at least one null character, '\0'. I illuminate this fact further in Chapter 6.

Exercises

1. The version of the program **sum1ton.c** shown on page 31 fails on a 16-bit system for all input and calculations exceeding 32767. Using **long int** definitions, the **atol** instead of the **atoi** conversion function and the **%ld** format codes in the second **printf**, modify the program so that it works with very large numbers.

2. Write a program that displays the fully-qualified file pathname C:\MSVC\BIN. If you're using UNIX, and prefer forward slashes, just humour me and do it with backslashes anyway.

3. Write a program that displays two literal strings, delimited by double-quotes in this way: "String1", "String2".

4. Write a program that defines a double variable to store the number 1.732050808 and then uses a loop to multiply the number by itself three times. Display the result. What do you get?

5. Write a program that defines two **char** variables, initialises them with the letters 'h' and 'g'. respectively. Add the variables together and display the result as a character. What do you get?

3 Functions

Organisation of a C program

Every C program is organised as a number of functions (including, exactly once, **main**) stored in at least one *program file*, or *translation unit*. Each program file should have a file name suffixed with **.c**. There can be as many program files as you like, collectively making up a whole C program. Here is a diagram that illustrates the organisation of a program made up of two program files:

```
//Program file progf1.c

#include <stdio.h>
#include "thisprog.h"

void func4(void)
{
    int x;
}
void main(void)
{
    func1();
    func5();
}
int func1(void)
{
    func2();
}
```

```
//Program file progf2.c

#include <stdio.h>
#include "thisprog.h"

void func5(void)
{
    func3();
}
void func2(void)
{

}
void func3(void)
{

}
```

Points to note:

- The functions do not have to be in any special order.

- There is exactly one **main** function, as there must be, regardless of the number of program files.

- Any function may call any other.

- Functions must not be *nested*: you can't define a function within a function.

- Function prototypes are not explicitly shown here, but are stored in the header file **thisprog.h**.

● In an #include line:

<angle brackets> are used for library headers files, and cause only the standard directories to be searched;

"double quotes" are used for your own header files, and cause the current directory to be searched in addition to the standard directories.

To build the program from the command-line, you issue this command in a UNIX session:

    cc progf1.c progf2.c

and the executable program is stored in **a.out**. In a DOS environment using the Borland C++ compiler, you issue this command:

    bcc progf1.c progf2.c

and the executable program becomes **progf1.exe**. Under Windows, using an IDE such as Visual C++, you construct a Project that includes the two program files and build the Project.

Function prototype, header and body

A function is a body of C code executed from another part of the program by a function call. Every function's definition consists of two parts, the header and a compound statement. You should also specify a function prototype, or declaration.

Prototype

A prototype is an announcement to the compiler of the existence in the program of a function definition with a header matching the prototype. When the function is called after the compiler has seen the prototype, the compiler can check that the form of the function call is correct.

Although it is not always strictly necessary, you should always declare all your functions in advance to the compiler using a prototype:

```
int power(int, int);      // function prototype
```

Make sure that the type of the return value and the number and types of arguments specified in the prototype exactly match those in the function header and in the call to the function.

Where you write many of your own functions, it's a good idea also to create your own header file (see **thisprog.h** in the previous section) and to store all the function prototypes there. Then you can **#include** the header file in all your program files, saving the bother of explicitly including the prototypes in every program file.

Header

A function header consists of a *return type*, the function name and the *parameter list*, also called an *argument list*, enclosed in parentheses. Look at these definitions and function call:

```
int result, num, n;
result = power(num, n);      // function call
```

The header of the called function is this:

```
int power(int num, int n)      // function header
```

In the header, the first **int** is the function's return type. This means that a value returned by the function to result is an integer. **int** is the default return type for functions. **power**, the function name, is an identifier, as the term is defined in Chapter 2. In the function call, the arguments **num** and **n** are copied to the parameters declared in the header of the called function **power**.

The function starts at the first character to the right of the opening parenthesis in the header. You can use the parameters enclosed in the parentheses inside the function in the same way as ordinary variables defined inside the function's main compound statement.

When you call the function, the values of the arguments used in the call to the function are copied into the parameters defined in the header. When control is returned from the called function to the statement following the function call, the values of the formal parameters are not returned. This means that an ordinary function cannot change the original values of arguments with which it is called.

If there are no arguments in the function call, you should explicitly specify their absence in both the prototype and the function header with the **void** keyword:

```
int power(void);  // prototype
result = power(); // call
int power(void)   // header
{
    // function body
}
```

This tells the compiler explicitly that the **power** function takes no parameters. If the call is made using arguments, the compiler reports an error.

Body

As you saw in Chapter 1, a function's body consists of a compound statement, a collection of statements enclosed in a pair of curly braces, {}. It's possible to precede the statements within the compound statement with data definitions, as you can see from this program, **power.c**, which contains a full definition of the **power** function:

power program and function

```c
/***********************************************************************
 *
 *    'power.c' —   Program to raise numbers to a specified power,
 *                  using a 'power' function.
 *
 ***********************************************************************/
#include <stdio.h>

long power(int, int);                         Function prototype

int main(void)
{
    int num, n;
    long result;

    printf("Enter number and exponent: ");
    scanf("%d %d", &num, &n);

    result = power(num, n);

    printf("%d to the power %d is %ld\n", num, n, result);

    return(0);
}

long power(int mantissa, int exponent)
{
    long result = (long)mantissa;

    while (exponent > 1)                      Function definition
    {
        result = result  * mantissa;
        exponent--;
    }
    return(result);
}
```

Here, **num** and **n** are copied from the function call to the parameters **mantissa** and **exponent** in **power**. **mantissa** and **exponent** are used within the function's body as easily as is the *local variable* result. When **mantissa** has been raised to the power **exponent**, the value of the exponentiation is returned in result to the point at which the function was called.

Notice that, although exponent is repeatedly decremented in **power**, its value in **main** after the function call is unchanged.

When you run the program, the display is similar to this:

    Enter number and exponent: **2 24**

    2 to the power 24 is 16777216

Data input is done using a library function you haven't seen before. **scanf** is essentially the reverse of **printf**; in this case calling it sets its arguments **num** and **n** to values that you input at the keyboard. If you're wondering why the address-of operator **&** is used with both these arguments, be patient. Call by reference is explained on page 48.

Return values and parameters

A function has two ways of returning information to the calling function: by return value and by parameters. As in the example of the **power** function, the **return** statement is used to return a value from a function to where the function was called.

If you use **return;** (without a value being returned) in a function, the result is unconditional return of control from the called function to the calling function. No particular value will be returned from the function in this case. It is more usual to use **return** to return control to the calling function with a value which is some use there. e.g.

```
return(FALSE);
return(ERR_NO);
return result;
```

The parentheses surrounding the returned values are optional.

The alternative to **return** for sending back information from a called function is use of parameters. All arguments passed between functions in C are copied. A call to a function passing arguments by value (copying them to the parameters declared in the header) is known as a *call by value*.

Call by value is the only method of argument passing used by C. C can also *simulate* passing arguments by reference (i.e., passing their addresses, not their values) using the address of (pointer to) the parameter data. A call to a function passing arguments by reference is known as a *call by reference*. (For more on this see the next section.)

The next program is a simple example, **addnos1.c**, of passing arguments to a function by value, returning the result to the point of call using a **return** statement. Calling a function to add two numbers smacks of overkill, but it demonstrates the argument-passing mechanism.

First, using **return**, the called function **add_nos** returns its data, converted to type **float**, to the floating-point variable **sum** in main. **add_nos** is supplied with its data from the arguments **x** and **y** specified in the function call in **main**. These values are copied to the formal parameters **a** and **b** in the header of **add_nos**. You don't have to use different names for the arguments in the function call and the

```
/*********************************************************************
 *
 *  'addnos1.c' — calls a function to add two numbers
 *                and sends back the result using 'return'.
 *
 *********************************************************************/
#include <stdio.h>

float add_nos(int, float);      // prototype

int main(void)
{
    int x = 14;
    float y = 3.162, sum;

    printf("Numbers in: %d %f\n", x, y);
    sum = add_nos(x, y);
    printf("Sum of %d and %6.3f is %6.3f\n", x, y, sum);
}
float add_nos(int a, float b)
{
    return(a+b);
}
```

parameters in the function header. The latter could be **x** and **y**; they are named differently here for clarity only.

In **main**, **x** is defined as an integer and **y** as a floating-point value. Their values are copied to **a** and **b** in **add_nos** which are defined with identical type. The arguments and parameters correspond by position. When you run the program, you get this:

```
Numbers in: 14 3.162000
Sum of 14 and  3.162 is 17.162
```

Take note

The types and order of the corresponding arguments and parameters must be the same.

Function call by reference

The distinction between call by value and call by reference is very important. *Call by value* means that the values of the arguments sent by the calling function are copied to the parameters received by the called function, and are not changed no matter what is done to the parameters in the called function. *Call by reference* means that the called function is using *the same data* as that sent by the calling function and *does* change the original values of the arguments.

The program **addnos1.c** uses a return value to pass back the result of the function **add_nos** to the point of its call in **main**. In this program, **addnos2.c**, the computed sum is returned to the calling function as the changed value of the second argument supplied to **add_nos**:

```
/************************************************************************
 *     'addnos2.c' – calls a function to add two numbers and
 *    sends back the result using pointers as parameters
 ************************************************************************/
#include <stdio.h>

void add_nos(int, float *);     // prototype

int main(void)
{
    int x = 14;
    float y = 3.162;
    float z = y;

    printf("Numbers in: %d %f\n", x, y);
    add_nos(x, &y);
    printf("Sum of %d and %6.3f is %6.3f\n", x, z, y);
}
void add_nos(int a, float *b)
{
    *b = *b + a;
    return;
}
```

The type of **y** and **b** is no longer a simple **float**, but a *pointer to float*. The second argument supplied to **add_nos** is no longer just **y**, but the *address of* (which means the same as *pointer to*) **y**. The value copied

50

to **b** is not the value of **y**, but a memory address for **y**. Altering the object at, or contents of, the pointer **b** in **add_nos**:

```
*b = *b + a;
```

does not change **b**, but the object to which **b** is pointing, namely the value of the original **y**. The value of **y** displayed by the second **printf** call in **main** reflects the change made by **add_nos**. The program's output is the same as that of **addnos1.c**.

To have a function change the value of a data object supplied to it as an argument, *the argument must be a pointer to the data object.* In the case of arrays, the name of an array is its address. An address is a pointer. So, if an array name is used as an argument in a function call, the called function can change the object at the pointer (the array's contents) such that the change is seen in the calling function.

Whenever you pass an array as an argument to a function, its contents may have changed when control is returned from the called function.

Let's look at an example where a function, **get_data**, is called with three array arguments. The purpose of the function is to accept data from the standard input and place that data in the arrays:

```
int get_data(char *, char *, char *); // prototype
int main(void)
{
    char dd[5],mm[5],yy[5];
    ...
    get_data(dd,mm,yy);
    ...
}

int get_data(char *dd, char *mm, char *yy)
{
    /* get_data function body */
}
```

The *addresses of* the three character arrays are copied to the variable names in the function header **get_data**. The three arrays may then be used within **get_data** in the ordinary way. If the values of the array elements are changed, the change affects their values in **main**.

Visibility of functions and data

If you define a variable within a function, it's a local variable, also called an *internal variable*. The local variable is of *automatic storage class* and only exists for the duration of execution of that function. It's also only visible, or *in scope*, for the code of that function.

On the other hand, a variable defined outside all functions (an *external*, or *global variable*) is of *static storage class* and exists for the duration of execution of the program. Making certain assumptions that I'll explain presently, an external variable is in scope for all the code in all functions in your program.

There are four storage class specifiers which you can use to specify explicitly a variable's storage class: **auto**, **register**, **static** and **extern**.

auto and register specifiers

For a variable to be of automatic storage class, it must be defined within a function. All the variables we have so far defined within functions are automatic, or **auto**, data objects.

This means that memory space for these variables is allocated each time the function is entered and that the space is discarded upon exit from the function. Because of this, an automatic variable cannot be accessed from any other function. The value of an automatic variable is lost on exit from the function in which it is defined. The integer definition

    int x;

means the same thing as

    auto int x;

if it is within a function and not otherwise qualified. However, **auto** is the default storage class specifier and need not be explicitly declared. (It rarely is.)

You can define a variable with the storage class specifier **register**. This is the same as **auto** in all ways except that the compiler, on seeing the **register** specifier, attempts to allocate space for the variable in a high-speed machine register, if such is available.

static storage class

You can define a variable with **static** storage class by placing it outside all functions or within a function prefixed with the keyword **static**. A static variable has its memory allocated at program compilation time, rather than in the transient manner of auto.

A static internal (defined within a function) variable retains its value even on exit from that function. A *static internal variable* cannot be accessed by other functions in the program – it is in scope only for the code of its own function – but a value assigned to it will still exist the next time the function is entered. An external variable is, by default, of static storage class.

If a static variable is not explicitly initialised, its value is set to zero at compile time, when space for it is allocated. Here is an example of how a static variable internal to a function retains its value even on exit from the function:

```
void run_total(void)
{
    static int total = 1;

    total = total + 1;
}
```

At compilation time, the compiler allocates space for **total** and sets its value to 1. This is done *only once*, not every time the function is entered. Every time the function is executed, the value of **total** is incremented by 1. The fourth time that the function is entered, the value of **total** is 4.

The extern specifier

The last storage class specifier is **extern**. An external variable may be accessed by any function in the program file in which it is defined. Its definition may be accessed by any function in another program file if it is declared in that program file with the prefix **extern**.

Here is an illustration of an **extern** declaration used in one program file to allow its code to access a global variable defined in another.

Functions are not variables, but they are external objects: they are accessible throughout the whole program. The start of a function is the first character to the right of the opening parenthesis, in front of the formal parameter declarations. All data objects declared within a function are internal. The function name is external because it is not part of the function itself. This in turn means that functions must not be nested.

Here is an example of a program consisting of two program files, **progf1.c** and **progf2.c**. It illustrates use of local variables, external (global) variables and the **extern** specifier.

```
// Program file progf1.c
// Global variable definition

int glob = 5;

int main(void)
{
    //glob visible here
}

void func1(void)
{
    //glob visible here
}
```

```
// Program file progf2.c
// Make global available

extern int glob;

void func2(void)
{
    // glob visible here too
}

void func3(void)
{
    // glob visible here too
}
```

This program is much the same in function as **nameaddr.c**, in Chapter 1. The major differences are that the function **dispdata** is now stored in a second program file. Two **extern** declarations are used, one to declare the **dispdata** function (this is not strictly necessary) and the other to allow **dispdata** access the global variable name.

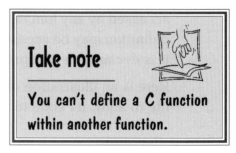

Take note

You can't define a C function within another function.

extern variables

```
/*************************************************************************
 *
 *      'progf1.c' – accept input of and display the user's name
 *       and address. Functions are split across two program files
 *
 *************************************************************************/
#include <stdio.h>

void getdata(char *, char *, char *);
void dispdata(char *, char *, char *);

// global variable
char name[20];

int main(void)
{
      //    Define variables to hold address data
      char addr1[30], addr2[30], addr3[30];

      //    Call function to accept keyboard input
      getdata(addr1, addr2, addr3);

      //    Call function to display the user-input data
      dispdata(addr1, addr2, addr3);

      //    Finished, stop program
      return(0);
}

void getdata(char *a1, char *a2, char *a3)
{
      printf("Enter name: ");
      gets(name);
      printf("Enter address 1: ");
      gets(a1);
      printf("Enter address 2: ");
      gets(a2);
      printf("Enter address 3: ");
      gets(a3);
}
```

```
/****************************************************************************
*
*       'progf2c' – accept input of and display the user's name
*          and address. Functions are split across two program files
*
*       ************************************************************************/
#include <stdio.h>

extern void dispdata(char *, char *, char *);

// Declaration of global defined elsewhere
extern char name[20];

void dispdata(char *addr1, char *addr2, char *addr3)
{
    printf("\nName and address details:\n\n");
    printf("\t%s\n", name);
    printf("\t%s\n", addr1);
    printf("\t%s\n", addr2);
    printf("\t%s\n", addr3);
}
```

You build the program at the command-line like this (I used the Borland C++ compiler):

```
bcc progf1.c progf2.c
```

and, when you run it (using the program name **progf1**), you get a display like this:

```
Enter name: Conor Sexton
Enter address 1: Rathfarnham
Enter address 2: Dublin
Enter address 3: Ireland

Name and address details:

    Conor Sexton
    Rathfarnham
    Dublin
    Ireland
```

Declaration and definition

The terms declaration and definition are often interchangeable but there is a crucial difference. A *declaration* specifies a data object with a name, type and storage class, but it does not allocate any space for the data in memory. A *definition* is a declaration which additionally allocates space for the data object.

A definition is a less general case of a declaration. *Every definition creates an instance in memory of a declaration.*

The places so far where we have seen a difference between declaration and definition are:

● Declaration of a function in advance to warn the compiler of its subsequent definition.

● In the case of external variables, definition of a global variable in one program file which is declared in other program file(s) by means of the extern storage class specifier.

One practical effect of the fact that declarations do not have memory allocated for them is that you can herd all your declarations together in a header file, and then **#include** the header file in all your program files. As no memory has been allocated, there is no risk of a double definition and consequent memory clash. Both function prototypes and extern declarations can be written into header files in this way.

Chapter 6 includes the rules for declaration of aggregate data types (including arrays and structures) and their definition as well as those for constructing, declaring and defining objects of original data types.

Take note

You must not put any definitions in your header file. Defining:

        int x;

in a header file is OK if the header file is only included in one program file.
As soon as it's included in two or more, you'll get linker errors.

Exercises

1. Write a program that, in its **main** function, repeatedly calls the function **run_total** with a single integer argument. The matching parameter in the header of **run_total** is called **increment**. Within the function, add **increment** to an accumulator and display the accumulator's value. That value should be the cumulative value for all the times **run_total** has so far been called.

2. Write a program that, in its **main** function, calls the function **get_num** with a single address-of-integer argument. **get_num** should read a number from the standard input. On return from **get_num**, display that number.

3. In the program **power.c** earlier in this chapter, the **scanf** library function is shown being supplied with the *addresses* of variables for its second and subsequent arguments. Why is this? Rewrite **ptrarg.c** to use **scanf** instead of the **atoi/gets** combination.

4 Expressions and operators

Boolean value of expressions

Every C expression has an inherent value, which is either zero or non-zero. In the philosophically-simple world of C, everything is either true or false. Zero is 'false'; non-zero is 'true'.

Unlike, for example, Pascal, C has no specific *boolean* data type. You have to use an **int** or **short** type if you want a boolean variable:

```
short   date_valid = 0;         // set FALSE
    ...
//   Assign return-value of date-validation function to the flag.
//   The return value is either 0 (FALSE) or 1 (TRUE).

date_valid = validate();

if (date_valid == 1)
    printf("Valid date entered.\n");
if (date_valid == 0)
    printf("Invalid date entered.\n");
```

With some preprocessor definitions, you can improve this code:

```
#define    boolean      short
#define    TRUE         1
#define    FALSE        0
    ...
boolean   date_valid = FALSE;

    ...
date_valid = validate();

if (date_valid == TRUE)
    printf("Valid date entered\n");
if (date_valid == FALSE)
    printf("Invalid date entered\n");
```

Recall that every expression has a zero or non-zero value. We can simplify the last four lines:

```
if (date_valid)
    printf("Valid date entered\n");
if (!date_valid)
    printf("Invalid date entered\n");
```

If **date_valid** is not zero, it is 'true' and the first test succeeds. If **date_valid** is zero, it is 'false'. The *unary negation operator*, !, causes the second test to go true and an invalid date is flagged.

In this example, the function call **validate()** is itself an expression with an inherent return value. It's OK to write:

```
if ((validate()) == TRUE)
    //   return value true, date valid
    printf("Valid date entered\n");
```

or simply:

```
if (validate())
    printf("Valid date entered\n");
```

You should be able to see from this process of reduction that C code is usually much 'tighter', or more concise, than code written in other languages. For example, in COBOL, you just can't embed a PERFORM statement (COBOL's approximate equivalent of a function call) in an IF test. But it's no problem (and is good practice) to do so in C.

For expressions, value zero represents 'false'; non-zero is 'true'. For relational expressions, 'false' equals zero and 'true' equals 1. To illustrate:

```
int     a = 0;
int     b = -5;
int     c = 5;
float   e = 2.71828;

a           //      FALSE
b           //      TRUE
a + b       //      TRUE
b + c       //      FALSE
e           //      TRUE

a == 0      //      TRUE (1)
b < 0       //      TRUE (1)
e > 3.0     //      FALSE (0)
```

Finally, the explicit values 1 and 0 may themselves be used to represent 'true' and 'false':

```
while (1)   //      infinite loop
while (!0)  //      same
```

Assignment

The simple assignment operator, =, changes the value of the operand to its left, sometimes called the *lvalue*. An lvalue must refer to a region of memory which the program may change. e.g. if **no_leaps** is an **int**:

```
no_leaps = 0;
```

To add 1 to the value of **no_leaps**, you can use the simple form:

```
no_leaps = no_leaps + 1;
```

This updates the **no_leaps** memory location with its current value plus one. It is more common (and better practice) to use the syntax:

```
no_leaps++;
```

This increments **no_leaps** by one. Depending on the compiler, the *post-increment* may lessen compile time and reduce resultant code output, as there is only one reference to the variable being incremented. Similarly, you can also write the decrement-by-one operation as:

```
no_leaps--;
```

To increment no_leaps by 2, you can use the expression:

```
no_leaps += 2;
```

This form of *compound assignment* can be generally applied:

```
x += y      is equivalent to    x = x + y
x *= y + z  is equivalent to    x = x * (y + z)
x /= y      is equivalent to    x = x / y
```

It is also legal to use the *prefix increment*:

```
++no_leaps;
```

If **no_leaps** is the only operand in the expression and this expression is not on the right-hand side of an assignment, this is equivalent to:

```
no_leaps++;
```

The uses of ++ before and after the variable are not always equivalent:

```
int days_total;
    ...
no_leaps = 5;
days_total = no_leaps++;
```

Here, the value of **days_total** after the assignment is 5. If you use:

```
days_total = ++no_leaps;
```

no_leaps is incremented then assigned to **days_total**, giving 6.

Comparing data

Relational operators

To compare the values of variables in your C programs, you need *relational operators*. The relational operators provided by C are:

<	less than	>	greater than
<=	less than or equal to	>=	greater than or equal to

The equality operators are:

==	equality	!=	non-equality

All arithmetic operations are done before relational tests, which in turn are carried out before tests for equality. For example:

    if (dd > MAXDD - 1)

means the same as

    if (dd > (MAXDD - 1))

though the second form clearer. Parentheses can help to eliminate surprises caused by unexpected effects of the precedence rules.

Logical operators

C's logical operators are:

&& AND	|| OR	! NOT

The precedence of the unary negation operator, !, is the same as that of unary minus, -, and is higher than any of the arithmetic, relational, or logical operators.

&& and || operations are of lower precedence than relational and equality operations. && is evaluated before ||. For example, evaluation of this *compound condition* will be unexpected:

    if (mm==4 || mm==6 || mm==9 || mm==11 && dd>30)

The first test is done for **mm** being equal to **4**. If **mm** is 4, 6 or 9, the test returns TRUE (1) whatever the value of **dd**.

To achieve what was probably required – if it's April, June, September or November AND the day is greater than 30 – use parentheses:

    if ((mm==4 || mm==6 || mm==9 || mm==11) && (dd > 30))

Conditional expressions

The conditional operator, **?:**, is the only so-called *ternary* operator implemented by the C language. The others are all either unary, in that the operator takes only one operand, or binary, taking two.

Using three operands, **?:** allows a shorthand to be used for **if....else** constructs such as:

```
if (x > y)
    max = x;
else
    max = y;
```

Using **?:** you can write this as:

```
max = (x > y) ? x : y;
```

The parentheses around the condition are not necessary; **?:** is of lower precedence than any of the arithmetic or logical operators.

Whether or not the condition expression is enclosed in parentheses, it is evaluated first. Depending on its boolean result one, and only one, of the second and third operands is evaluated.

One of the major uses of the **?:** operator is for defining *preprocessor macros*. **?:** allows macros to be defined on one line and may cause the compiler to generate more efficient code than the **if....else** equivalent:

```
#define MAX(A, B) (A > B) ? A : B
```

After you make this preprocessor definition, all subsequent uses of MAX (for example MAX(5, 6)) are substituted in your program's code with the expression:

```
(A > B) ? A : B
```

which, in the example, evaluates to:

```
(5 > 6) ? 5 : 6
```

and eventually, 6.

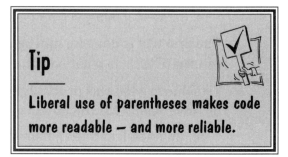

Tip

Liberal use of parentheses makes code more readable — and more reliable.

Precedence and associativity

C's rules of precedence and associativity determine the order in which the operations are evaluated in an expression. From the conventions of simple arithmetic, you would expect **a * b + c** to be evaluated as **(a * b) + c** and not **a * (b + c)**. Some conventions hold that division is of higher precedence than multiplication, but in C they are the same, along with the modulus operator %.

Addition and subtraction are of the same precedence relative to each other, but lower than the other arithmetic operators.

Associativity is subordinate to precedence: when two operators are of the same precedence, the order of evaluation of the expression is controlled by their associativity.

The expression following the definitions uses all of the multiplicative operators, which are of equal precedence and associate left-to-right:

```
int a = 10;
int b = 5;
int c = 9;
int d = 4;

a / b * c%d        // 10/5*9%4: result is 2
```

You can now examine the full table of operator precedence and associativity. A few operators are included that you haven't seen yet. These are mainly concerned with advanced use of pointers, where precedence of pointer operators becomes important.

Unary -, + and * are of higher precedence than the same operators used with binary operands.

The () operator means the parentheses in a function call.

The [ ] operator means array-bound square brackets.

Operators -> and . are the pointer-to and member-of operators for structures, which are described in Chapter 6.

The last operator in the table is the *comma operator*. This is infrequently used. When it is used, it separates two expressions, guaranteeing that the second expression is evaluated after the first.

Operators	Associativity
( ) [ ] -> .	left to right
! ~ ++ — + - * & (type) sizeof	right to left
* / %	left to right
+ -	left to right
<< >>	left to right
< > <= >=	left to right
== !=	left to right
&	left to right
^	left to right
|	left to right
&&	left to right
||	left to right
?:	right to left
= += -= *= /= %= &= ^= |= <<= >>=	right to left
,	left to right

The asterisk, ***** doubles as the multiplication operator and the *pointer-dereferencing* (object at a pointer) operator.

& is the address-of operator, which is unary and returns the address of the variable following.

If you can remember the order of precedence and associativity for all operators in C, fine. Otherwise, *use parentheses*, even if they are not strictly necessary. It costs nothing to use the parentheses. It also saves errors and improves code readability.

Example: validating a date

This section introduces the first program presented in this book that is actually useful. The program is called **validate.c** and does a job that every programmer in every language seems to have to do about 62 times in their life: checking that a given date is valid. For simplicity, a 20th-century input of form dd/mm/yy is assumed (I'm now storing up my own year-2000 problem!). First, we write a header file, **dates.h**, that defines necessary preprocessor symbolic constants and holds function prototypes:

```
/*********************************************************************
 *
 *      'dates.h'
 *
 *********************************************************************/
#define MINYY   0
#define MAXYY   99
#define MINYY   0
#define MINMM   1
#define MAXMM   12
#define MINDD   1
#define MAXDD   31
#define MINFEB  28
#define MAXFEB  29
#define TRUE    1
#define FALSE   0

// Function prototype declarations follow
void  get_data(int *, int *, int *);
int  validate(int, int, int);
```

Next, the program file **validate.c**, which contains the validation logic:

```
/*********************************************************************
 *
 *      'validate.c' – accepts as input a date of form dd/mm/yy,
 *      validates the date, and returns the result of the validation.
 *
 *********************************************************************/
#include <stdio.h>
#include <stdlib.h>
#include "dates.h"
```

```c
int main(void)
{
    int c, yy, mm, dd;

    get_data(&dd, &mm, &yy);

    // Check date for correctness. 20th century date assumed.
    if (validate(dd, mm, yy))
        printf ("Date entered is valid\n\n");
    else
        printf ("Invalid date entered\n\n");
    return(0);
}

void get_data(int *pdd, int *pmm, int *pyy)
{
    printf("Enter a date of form dd/mm/yy: ");
    scanf("%d/%d/%d",pdd, pmm, pyy);
}

int validate(int dd, int mm, int yy)
{
    //    Validate the date according to the well-known rules

    if ((yy < MINYY) || (yy > MAXYY))
        return (FALSE);
    if ((mm < MINMM) || (mm > MAXMM))
        return (FALSE);
    if ((dd < MINDD) || (dd > MAXDD))
        return (FALSE);
    if ((mm==4) || (mm==6) || (mm==9) || (mm==11))
        if (dd > (MAXDD - 1))
            return (FALSE);

    //    If the month is February and the year is divisible evenly
    //    by 4, we have a leap year, unless the year is 00.
    //    1900 was not a leap year; 2000 is.

    if (mm == 2)
    {
        if (dd > MAXFEB)
            return(FALSE);
```

```
        if (((yy % 4) != 0) || (yy == MINYY))
            if (dd > MINFEB)
                return(FALSE);
    }

    //    valid date
    return(TRUE);
}
```

Two functions are called from **main**: **get_data** and **validate**. **get_data** does what its name suggests; it prompts the user for input of three numbers, which are then treated as day, month and year respectively. **get_data** must set its parameters to the user-input data and the changed parameter values must be available in main after the call to **get_data**. To achieve this, **get_data** is called by reference: addresses of the arguments are used, not their values. Within **get_data**, the **scanf** library function accepts data from the user into the memory at those addresses.

After the input date has been read by **get_data**, the three numbers are passed (by value) to validate for checking. There should be no need here to go in detail through the logic of validate; it's pretty clear and you should be able to understand it without further explanation. Depending on the TRUE/FALSE status returned by validate, a message confirming the validity, or not, of the date is output from main. Here's the screen output of two runs of the program:

```
Enter a date of form dd/mm/yy: 29/2/93
Invalid date entered

Enter a date of form dd/mm/yy: 29/2/92
Date entered is valid
```

validate.c pulls together in one program many of the important aspects of C syntax that you have seen so far in this book.

69

Exercises

1. Write a program that implements a preprocessor macro to display the minimum of two integer numbers.

2. The following variation of the function validate fails. Why?

```
int validate(int yy, int mm, int dd)
{
    //    Validate the date entered according to the well-known rules

    if ((yy < MINYY) || (yy > MAXYY))
        return (FALSE);
    if ((mm < MINMM) || (mm > MAXMM))
        return (FALSE);
    if ((dd < MINDD) || (dd > MAXDD))
        return (FALSE);
    if (mm==4 || mm==6 || mm==9 || mm==11 && (dd > (MAXDD - 1)))
        return (FALSE);

    //   If the month is February and the year is divisible evenly by 4,
    //   we havea leap year, unless the year is 00.
    //   1900 was not a leap year; 2000 is.
    if (mm == 2)
    {
        if (dd > MAXFEB)
            return(FALSE);
        if (((yy % 4) != 0) || (yy == MINYY))
            if (dd > MINFEB)
                return(FALSE);
    }

    //    valid date
    return(TRUE);
}
```

3. What happens when this statement is executed?

```
while (c = getchar() != 'q')
```

4. Modify **validate.c** so that it checks for correctness all dates in the range 00 (year zero) to 9999. Be aware that 3 – 13 September 1752 (inclusive) were lost in the switch from the Julian to the Gregorian calendar. Also, years divisible with zero remainder by 4 AND by 400 are leap years; years divisible evenly by 100 but NOT by 400 are not leap years. 1900 was therefore NOT a leap year.

5 Branching and looping

Program structure

In Chapter 3, you saw that the body of a function following the function header is a compound statement or statement block.

C is a *block-structured language*. It encourages programs to be written according to the rather loosely-defined principles of *structured programming*.

In the original definitions of languages such as COBOL and FORTRAN, there was no inherent structured approach. Change in the order of execution of statements in the program (control flow) was accomplished using an unconditional branch statement (GOTO) or a subroutine call (such as CALL, PERFORM).

Unstructured control flow makes for unreadable code. This is inefficient, prone to errors on the part of the programmer and, as an unstructured program grows, increasingly difficult to maintain.

The following are some simple principles of the structured programming approach:

- Programs are designed in a top-down manner; the major functions required for the solution are called from the highest-level function. Each of the called functions further refines the solution and calls further functions as necessary.

- Each function is short and carries out one logical task.

- Every function is as independent as possible of all other functions. Information is exchanged between functions via arguments and return values. Use of global variables and shared code is minimised.

- Unconditional branching is avoided.

C provides the facilities necessary to meet these objectives.

- All statements are either simple statements - expressions terminated by semicolons - or compound statements, which are statement groups enclosed by curly braces {}. A compound statement is syntactically equivalent to a simple statement.

- Every C program must have a **main** function from which, ideally, functions dealing with the highest level of the solution are called. It is sometimes held that no function should be longer than 50 lines of code; if it is, it should be broken down into a calling and one or more called functions.

- Using function return values and arguments, C allows you to exchange data between functions to an extent which minimises the use of global variables.

- C provides a goto statement for unconditional branching, but its use and power are severely restricted.

- C provides a range of statements for control of program execution flow. These are all based on switching control between the program's constituent compound statements and, collectively, they allow you to write concise, logically-structured programs.

if

The general form of the **if** statement is this:

```
if (<expression>)
    <statement1>
[else
    <statement2>]
```

The square brackets indicate that the **else** clause is optional.

The expression may be any legal expression, including an assignment, function call or arithmetic expression. The inherent boolean value of the expression determines change, if any, made to the program's flow of control by the **if** statement.

The statements subject to the **if** and the **else** may be any legal single or compound statement. If a single statement is subject to an **if** or **else**, use of the compound-statement delimiters {} is optional; for two or more statements they are necessary. For example, when **getchar** reads the letter 'q' from the keyboard, we can stop program execution:

```
if ((c = getchar()) == 'q')
{
    // Finish program execution

    printf("Program terminating\n");
    return(0);
}
```

You can nest **if** statements and the optional **else** clauses to any depth:

```
if (mm == 2)
    if (((yy %4) != 0) > (yy == MINYY))
        if (dd > MINFEB)
            return(FALSE);
```

What does this triple-nested if mean? If the month is February AND (if the year is not a leap year OR the year is 1900) AND if the day is greater than 28, there is an error.

Each **if** statement, including its subject compound statement(s), is syntactically a single statement. This is why the last example, although it contains three nested **if** statements, is a single statement; no compound statement delimiters, {}, are necessary.

You can use the delimiters if you like:

```
if  (mm == 2)
{
    if (((yy %4) != 0) > (yy == MINYY))
    {
        if (dd > MINFEB)
            return(FALSE);
    }
}
```

This makes no difference at all to the logic but gives an improvement in code readability. Use of compound-statement braces becomes important when the else option is used.

```
if (mm == 2)
    if (((yy %4) != 0) > (yy == MINYY))
        if (dd > MINFEB)
            return(FALSE);
else
    return(TRUE);      //    valid date
```

Each **else** corresponds to the last **if** statement for which there is no other **else**, unless forced to correspond otherwise by means of {} braces. In this example, the **else** refers to the third **if**, although it is presumably intended to correspond with the first. To get the result you probably want, write this:

```
if (mm == 2)
{
    if (((yy %4) != 0) > (yy == MINYY))
        if (dd > MINFEB)
            return(FALSE);
}
else
    return(TRUE);      //    valid date
```

Lastly, you can nest to any depth the whole **if...else** construct itself:

```
if (dd == 1)
    printf("Monday\n");
else
if (dd == 2)
    printf("Tuesday\n");
```

```
else
if (dd == 3)
    printf("Wednesday\n");
else
if (dd == 4)
    printf("Thursday\n");
else
if (dd == 5)
    printf("Friday\n");
else
if (dd == 6)
    printf("Saturday\n");
else
if (dd == 0)
    printf("Sunday\n");
else
    printf ("Error\n");
```

This is a multi-way decision. The construct is more efficient than it would be if all the **if** statements were used without **else** clauses. As it stands, as soon as an individual test is successful, execution of the whole sequence stops. If **dd** is not in the 0 – 6 range, the last **else** does processing for the 'none of the above' case and flags an error.

There is a special facility in C for more efficiently handling cases like this: I explain the **switch** statement on page 84.

Loops

On page 18, I described the basic rules governing the while and for loops. The examples given there both increase, in steps of 1, the value of a variable from 1 to 99 inclusive.

Here is similar code written with a **do ... while** construct:

```
int x = 1;

do
{
    printf("Number %d\n", x),
    x = x + 1;

} while (x < 100);
```

The **for** and the while loop types are equivalent. The **do-while** variant in this case is equivalent in effect to the other two, but notice that the body of the loop is always executed once, whatever the value of **x**. This is useful for some purposes, for example, if you want a menu to display at least once, but can have unintended side effects.

Note that you must terminate the **do-while** condition with a semicolon.

The examples illustrate that, in most situations, one of the three loop types will be particularly suitable. In general, the **for** loop suits cases where the limits to the number of iterations are known in advance. This is the case in traversing an array with fixed subscript limits and in reading a data file until end-of-file. Where the increment step code is lengthy, as in the case above, the **for** loop is cumbersome.

It is always possible to use **while** and **for** interchangeably, but **while** is usually suitable in those cases where **for** is not.

All three loop statements are syntactically single statements. You can nest them to any level without using compound statement delimiters:

```
for (i=0;i<100 && arr1[i];i++)
    for (j=0;j<100 && arr2[j];i++)
        if (arr1[i] == arr2[j])
            return(i);
```

This code traverses two 100-element arrays looking for matching elements. It is all one statement, hence the absence of curly braces.

Unconditional branch statements

There are four unconditional-branch statements available in C. In ascending order of power, they are: **continue**, **break**, **return**, **goto**.

break

You can use **break** to exit early from any type of loop or from a **switch** statement. Let's define a **char** array of ten elements and a subscript:

```
char arr[10];
int sub;
```

Assume the array has been initialised with a string. We traverse the array, display each character and exit the loop on encountering '\0':

```
for (sub = 0; sub < 10; sub++)
{
    if (arr[sub] == '\0')
        break;
    printf("%c",arr[sub]);
}
```

The **break** causes unconditional exit from the loop. Control is passed to the first statement after the loop's compound statement. **break** only causes exit from one level of loop; if the loops are nested, control is returned from the loop containing the **break** to the outer loop.

continue

continue passes control to the loop's controlling expression or the increment step of a **for** loop. If the loop does not terminate naturally, the next iteration is performed. **continue** can only be used within loop statements. Let's traverse the array again. If '\n' is encountered, it is ignored and the characters, stripped of newlines, are displayed.

```
sub = -1;
while (sub < 10)
{
    sub++;
    if (arr[sub] == '\n')
        continue;
    printf("%c",arr[sub]);
}
```

There is a danger in using **continue**. As it causes part of an iteration to be skipped, problems arise if the loop-control variable is updated during this part. In this case, if **sub** were incremented after the **printf**

– as in ordinary code it might well be – it would fail to be incremented for the first '\n' encountered. You would get an infinite loop.

goto

goto transfers control unconditionally to the point in the code marked by a named label followed by a colon. **goto** can be useful but is never necessary. Anything that you can do with **goto** you can do with other flow-control statements, and **goto** tends to lead to unreadable code. However, there are a few cases where it serves a purpose.

break causes exit from one loop to the first statement after the loop. **return** causes control to be returned from a function to the calling function. Where loops are nested, there is no ready way to transfer control from the innermost loop to a point outside all the nested loops but without leaving the function.

Here is a reasonable use of **goto**. We define two character arrays and two subscript variables:

```
char arr1[100], arr2[100];
int i,j;
```

We want to find a character in **arr2** that is also in **arr1** and then exit.

```
for (i=0;i<100 && arr1[i];i++)
{
    for (j=0;j<100 && arr2[j];j++)
    {
        if (arr1[i] == arr2[j])
            goto match;
    }
}
printf("No match found\n");
goto end;
match: printf("Match found %c\n",arr1[i]);
end:      ;        // null statement
```

The **goto** label is only visible within the function containing the **goto** statement. You can therefore only use **goto** within one function. **goto** should not be used to transfer control to a statement within a loop. If the loop-control variables have already been initialised, use of **goto** to a point in the middle of the loop may bypass that initialisation and the loop will go out of control, probably with unpleasant results.

Multi-case selection

As I've already pointed out, C provides a statement to handle the special case of a multi-way decision. Here is the **switch** implementation of the **if...else...if** multi-way decision given earlier in this chapter.

```
switch(dd)
{
    case 1: printf("Monday\n");
            break;
    case 2: printf("Tuesday\n");
            break;
    case 3: printf("Wednesday\n");
            break;
    case 4: printf("Thursday\n");
            break;
    case 5: printf("Friday\n");
            break;
    case 6: printf("Saturday\n");
            break;
    case 0: printf("Sunday\n");
            break;
    default: printf("Error\n");
            break;
}
```

Execution control is switched, depending on the value of the variable **dd**. The variable must be of one of the integer types or of type char. Each of the expected values of **dd** is enumerated. If **dd** is one of those values, the code adjacent to the **case** label is executed. The **case** values must be constants. All **case** expressions in a given **switch** statement must be unique.

switch in C provides entry points to a block of statements. When control is transferred to a given entry point, execution starts at the first statement after that entry point. Unless directed otherwise, execution will simply fall through all code following, even though that code is apparently associated with other case labels.

For this reason, you need to insert a **break** at the end of the statements subject to a **case** label unless you want all the code within the **switch** block, starting from a given **case** label, to be executed.

In the example above, if all the **break** statements were left out and **dd** had the value 3, control would fall through the **switch** statement to the end and messages for all the days from Wednesday through to Sunday would be displayed. Omit **break** statements from switch at your peril!

If you use **break** in a **switch** statement, it causes control to be transferred completely out of the **switch** statement. **continue** does not apply to **switch**; it only has any effect if the **switch** statement is embedded in a loop.

The **default** case prefixes code which is executed if none of the previous **case** conditions is true. You should end the statements subject to default with a **break**. Inclusion of the **default** case is optional. There must be only one **default** in a **switch** statement (or none). **default** may occur anywhere in a **switch** statement, but is usually placed at the end.

If the statements labelled by a **case** immediately preceding the **default** label are executed, control will fall through to the **default** label unless a **break** statement is encountered.

You can nest **switch** statements to any depth. A **case** or **default** label is part of the smallest **switch** that encloses it.

The next page shows a somewhat contrived program, **jumpstmt.c**, notable mainly for the fact that it succeeds in using all the unconditional branch statements together:

At the start of the **main** function, the user is prompted to enter a number intended to represent a day of the week. When the user presses RETURN, newline (**\n**) and carriage return (**\r**) characters are also generated at the keyboard, so the program discards those by using **continue** to go back to the top of the loop and get another character. If the character is not in the range zero to 9, the code transfers control to the top of the loop.

Finally, there is a **switch** statement. Cases 8 and 9 are discarded as invalid. The **default** case (which need not be at the end of the **switch**) uses a **goto** to transfer control to the label **finish** and a message proclaiming input of zero to be invalid.

After the **switch** construct, another **goto** is used to jump over the **finish** label; this gives an insight to the kind of spaghetti code you can generate using **goto**s, if you're not careful.

unconditional branching

```
/***********************************************************************
 *
 *      'jumpstmt.c' — repeatedly accepts as input a character
 *      and tests it for being a number in the range 1-7
 *      representing the day of the week.
 *
 ***********************************************************************/
#include <stdio.h>

int main(void)
{
    int c;

    printf("Enter a number: ");
    while ((c = getchar()) != EOF)
    {
        if ((c == '\n') || (c == '\r'))
            continue;
        if ((c < '0') || (c > '9'))
        {
            printf("You must enter a single-digit number\n");
            printf("Enter a number: ");
            continue;
        }
        switch(c)
        {
            case '8':
            case '9': printf("Number not in range 1-7\n");
                break;
            default:  goto finish;
            case '1': printf("Monday\n");
                break;
```

```
                case '2': printf("Tuesday\n");
                    break;
                case '3': printf("Wednesday\n");
                    break;
                case '4': printf("Thursday\n");
                    break;
                case '5': printf("Friday\n");
                    break;
                case '6': printf("Saturday\n");
                    break;
                case '7': printf("Sunday\n");
                    break;
            }
            printf("Enter a number: ");
        }
        goto returnnow;
finish:
        printf("Zero invalid, program terminating...\n");
returnnow:
    return 0;
}
```

When you run the program and enter data as prompted, you get a screen display something like this:

```
Enter a number: 5
Friday
Enter a number: 4
Thursday
Enter a number: 9
Number not in range 1-7
Enter a number: 0
Zero invalid, program terminating...
```

Exercises

1. Using each of the three loop forms, write infinite loops.

2. Write a program that presents a simple menu of five numbered items and then waits for the user to enter a number selecting one of them. Display acknowledgement of the selection or report an error if the selection is not in the range 1 – 5.

3. Write a program that, for the years 0000 to 9999, finds the *day of the date* for a date input either as the three separate numbers *dd, mm* and *yy* (19/11/96) or as *dd, mm* and *ccyy.* (19/11/1996)

   This is not a trivial problem: allow yourself several hours.

6 Arrays and structures

Defining and initialising arrays

Definition

Here is a definition of an array of data objects of type **int**:

    int   numbers[10];

Ten integer data objects are defined. They are individually accessed by means of the identifier numbers suffixed by a subscript enclosed in square brackets.

numbers[0] is the first (element zero), leftmost integer in the array.
numbers[1] is the second.
...
numbers[9] is the last, or rightmost, element.

Subscripts in C always start at zero and stop one short of the subscript limit given in the array definition. Subscript values at the time of array definition must be constants. C does not allow variable-bound array definitions. You can define arrays of objects of any data type. Both the following are fine:

    char   charray[20];
    float   flarray[50];

You can also define arrays of pointers and arrays of aggregate data types, including arrays, structures and other, programmer-defined, data objects.

Here is a definition of a multi-dimensional array – an array of arrays:

    int   matrix[20][15];

matrix[20][15]

[0][0]	[0][14]
[1][0]	[1][14]
[19][0]	[19][14]

Take note

You can define arrays in any number of dimensions. If you find it easy to use arrays of four or more dimensions, then your intelligence is superior to mine.

Considering the array **matrix**:

- There are 20 rows, counted from zero to 19.

- There are 15 columns, counted from zero to 14.

- **matrix[14][11]** can be thought of as the element at row 14, column 11.

- **matrix[14][11]** is more accurately thought of as the 11th element of array 14.

- The array matrix is not, in fact, organised in memory as a rectangle of integer data objects; it is a contiguous line of integers treated as 20 sets of 15 elements each:

- The subscripts of matrix are specified in row-column order – **matrix[r][c]** – and the column subscript varies more rapidly than the row subscript, in line with the way in which the array elements are stored in memory.

Initialisation

You can explicitly initialise an array using an *initialiser list* consisting entirely of constant values. Any initial values of automatic array elements that are not explicitly initialised are garbage; for static arrays, the array elements are zero.

You can enclose array initialiser lists in curly braces, as in the example below, or, in the case of string initialisation, use a string literal enclosed by double quotes.

You could define and initialise an array, **mdd**, to hold the number of days in each month of the year:

```
int mdd[13] = {0,31,28,31,30,31,30,31,31,30,31,30,31};
```

The data used to initialise an array must be a set of constants enclosed in curly braces, separated by commas and terminated with a semicolon.

In the same way, you could set up a character array:

```
char    arr[5] = {'h','e','l','l','o'};
```

If there are more initialising data objects within the curly braces than implied by the subscript limit, the compiler reports an error. If there are fewer initialising data objects than the subscript limit, all excess elements in the array are set to zero.

You initialise two- and multi-dimensional arrays like this:

```
int  tab[3][4] = {
             {1,2,3,4},
             {5,6,7,8},
             {9,10,11,12}
             };
```

Here the outside curly braces are necessary, while the internal ones are optional but are included for readability. The first array bound, [3], is the number of rows and the second, [4], represents the number of columns. The array **tab** consists of three four-element integer arrays. The contents of some of its elements are:

```
tab[0][0]   ==   1
tab[1][2]   ==   7
tab[2][3]   ==   12
```

You can leave out one of the array bounds, but not both:

```
int  tab[][4] = {
             {1,2,3,4},
             {5,6,7,8},
             {9,10,11,12}
             };
```

Strings, subscripts and pointers

Definition of string

Strings are arrays of elements of type **char** terminated by the first null character, '\0', in the array. The definition from the last section:

    char   arr[5] = {'h','e','l','l','o'};

is a *character array*; elements 0 to 4 of the array are initialised with the five letters of 'hello'. The definition:

    char arr[6] = {'h','e','l','l','o','\0'};

is a *string* initialised to 'hello' and null-terminated. To accommodate the null character, the second definition of **arr** needs one more element. *Forgetting that the null character takes up one array element is a source of some difficult bugs.* The last definition is equivalent to:

char arr[6] = "hello";

A character constant, which can only represent one character, is delimited by single quotes as in 'a' and '\n'. A string literal is delimited by double quotes. Double quotes imply the existence of a terminating null character.

The single-quoted sequence 'a' is the mechanism used in C to represent the ASCII code-table entry for the letter 'a'. By contrast, "a" is a null-terminated string, equivalent to the character pair 'a','\0'.

You can use string literals in the same way as variable strings, and even access single characters of a string literal by using a subscript:

    "hello"[1] == 'e'

Each time you use a string literal in a program, the compiler may allocate new memory space for it – an *unnamed static array* – even if it is identical to a string literal used earlier in the program. By contrast, a variable array, once defined either externally or internally, will only have one memory allocation made for it at any given time. You shouldn't use an error message such as:

    "Error: can't open file"

repeatedly in a program in its string-literal form. Instead, it's best to use the literal to initialise a variable and then to use the variable with successive **printf** calls.

Finding string length using subscripts

This program, **slengths.c**, calculates the length (counting from 1, not zero) of a string. The call to **slength** – which traverses the string to find its length – is included as part of the second **printf** statement in **main**. Every function has a return value and type. **slength** is of type **int**, so the call to it is treated as an **int** in the **printf** statement.

```
/**********************************************************************
 *
 *      'slengths.c' – find the length of a string stored in
 *      a character array, using subscripts
 *
 *      ********************************************************************/
#include <stdio.h>

int slength(char []);

int main(void)
{
        char instring[50];
        printf("Enter input string ");
        gets(instring);
        printf("String length is %d\n", slength(instring));
        return(0);
}

int slength(char instring[])
{
        int i;

        for (i=0; instring[i] != '\0'; i++)
                ;
        return(i);
}
```

> Loops to the '\0' at the end of the string, counting as it goes.

> This is a null statement – all the work is done in the **for** line.

slength traverses the array until a null character is encountered, counting the number of characters on the way. The body of the **for** loop doing this consists of just a semicolon, which is a *null statement*.

The counting of characters includes the null character '\0'. Normally, the null character is not included in a string's length. However, we want to report the string's length as if we were counting from 1, not zero. Counting in the null character compensates for the fact that we are counting from zero. Here's the output when the program is run:

Enter input string **Out damned spot!**
String length is 16

If the string is not terminated with a null character, **slength** will run on until it reaches the end of the system's memory or it is stopped by the operating system. C does not check for this and all kinds of ghastly errors can result from omitting string terminators.

Finding string length using pointers

Given these definitions:

```
char        stg[50];
char        *cptr, *lptr;
```

and initialising the pointers:

```
cptr = lptr = stg;
```

the code following finds the length of the string, assuming the string is initialised and null-terminated:

```
while (*lptr)
    lptr++;
return(lptr - cptr);
```

This is part of the pointer version of the **slength** function, which is given in full below. Remember:

- **cptr** and **lptr** point at the address of the first element of the array **stg**.

- ***lptr** is the contents of that element.

- ***lptr** is the same as **stg[0]**.

- **lptr** is the same as **&stg[0]**.

When **lptr** is incremented by one, ***lptr** is equivalent to **stg[1]**; when further incremented by one, ***lptr** is the same as **stg[2]**, and so on.

lptr is incremented until its contents (***lptr**) equal the null character. If ***lptr** is null, it is inherently false, so you don't have to make an explicit comparison between it and '\0'. The displacement of the pointer **lptr** from the array address **stg** (same as **cptr**) is calculated by subtraction, giving the length of the string **stg**.

Here is the pointer version of the string-length program, **slengthp.c**:

```
/******************************************************************
 *
 *      'slengthp.c' — Program to find the length of a string stored in
 *                    a character array, using pointers
 *
 ******************************************************************/
#include <stdio.h>

int slength(char *);

int main(void)
{
    char instring[50];
    char *cptr = instring;

    printf("Enter input string ");
    gets(cptr);
    printf("String length is %d\n", slength(cptr));
    return(0);
}

int slength(char *cptr)
{
    char *lptr = cptr;

    while (*lptr)
        lptr++;
    return(lptr - cptr);
}
```

> The integer number returned by **slength** to **main** is the displacement between the two pointers **lptr** and **cptr** and is the length of the string **instring**.

Library functions for strings

Common operations on strings include copying, length-checking and comparison. Using the standard header file, string.h, you can use the C Library functions for string-handling. To use **string.h**, you should include it in your program using the preprocessor:

    #include <string.h>

Some of the most often-used string functions are:

strlen	Finds the length of a string
strcat	Joins two strings
strcpy	Copies one string to another
strcmp	Compares two strings
strncmp	Compares parts of two strings

strlen operates like **slengths** and **slengthp** from the previous section:

    int len;
    char   s[50] = "A text string";

    len = strlen(s);

After this code, **len** contains the number of characters in the string (13), not counting the terminating null character.

strcat concatenates two strings:

    char s1[50] = "A text string ";
    char s2[50] = "with another appended";

    strcat(s1, s2);

This appends the string **s2** to the string **s1**, yielding "*A text string with another appended*" as the contents of **s1**. It's your responsibility to ensure that **s1** is long enough to accommodate the joined strings. In real applications, the first argument to **strcat** is usually a pointer pointing to enough dynamically-allocated memory to ensure that both strings can be stored. (See Chapter 7 for more on this.)

strcpy copies the second string operand to the first, stopping after the null character has been copied. The next example shows its use.

strcmp and **strncmp** both compare two strings and return a negative, zero or positive value, depending on whether the first string is alphabetically less than, equal to or greater than the second.

```
        char s1[50], s2[50];

        strcpy(s1, "hello");
        strcpy(s2, "hallo");

        result = strcmp(s1, s2);// s1 greater than s2, so result is positive
```

strncmp does the same thing as **strcmp**, but only compares a specified number of characters in the two strings:

```
        strncmp(s1, s2, 1);
```

This would compare only the first letters of the two strings and would return a zero value, denoting equality. You cannot compare two strings using the == equality operator. Each character in the two strings must be compared to its counterpart in the other string. The library functions **strcmp** and **strncmp** are provided for this purpose.

Example: pattern matching

strpos.c, accepts as input two strings **s1** and **s2** and finds the start position in **s1** of **s2**. If **s2** is not found in **s1**, a negative value is returned. The **strpos** function, which finds the position of **s2** in **s1**, is extremely useful for pattern matching in text. Its C-library equivalent is **strstr**.

```
/***********************************************************
 *
 *       'strpos.c' – find the position of string s2 in s1. It returns
 *       the position if found, or a negative value otherwise.
 *
 ***********************************************************/
#include <stdio.h>
#include <string.h>
#define MAX 50

int strpos(char *, char *);

int main(void)
{
    char    str1[MAX], str2[MAX];
    char    *s1 = str1, *s2 = str2;
    int     pos;
```

```
        printf("Enter string to be searched: ");
        gets(s1);
        printf("Enter search string: ");
        gets(s2);
        pos = strpos(s1, s2);
        if (pos < 0)
            printf("%s not found in %s", s2, s1);
        else
            printf("%s at position %d in %s", s2,pos,s1);
        return(0);
}
int strpos(char *s1, char *s2)
{
        int    len;
        char   *lptr = s1;

        len  = strlen(s2);
        while (*lptr)
        {
            if ((strncmp(lptr, s2, len)) == 0)
                return(lptr - s1 + 1);
            lptr++;
        }
        return(-1);
}
```

> equivalent to
>
> while (***lptr** != NULL)
>
> keeps looping as long as **lptr** points at a non-null character.

> If no match is found, **strpos** returns the position as -1.

Here's how the function **strpos** works. Suppose **s1** points to the string "*Great Dunsinane he strongly fortifies*" (more Shakespeare!), while **s2** points to the string "*Dunsinane*". The function first sets a pointer, **lptr**, equal to **s1** and thus pointing at the longer string. A call to **strlen** finds the length of the string at **s2** which in this case is 9. Inside the loop, **strncmp** is used to compare "*Dunsinane*" with successive 9-character substrings of the longer string. If there's a match, **strncmp** returns zero and **strpos** returns the position of "Dunsinane", that is, 7.

Here's the display produced by **strpos.c**:

```
Enter string to be searched: Great Dunsinane he strongly fortifies
Enter search string: Dunsinane
Dunsinane at position 7 in Great Dunsinane he strongly fortifies
```

Structures

The elements of an array are all the same size and type. If you need to group together in one entity data objects of different sizes and types, you can use structures to do so. A structure is an aggregate data type: a collection of variables referenced under one name. A structure declaration is a *programmer-defined data type*.

Declaring a structure

Here is an example of a structure declaration:

```
struct stock_type
{
    char    item_name[30];
    char    part_number[10];
    double  cost_price;
    double  sell_price;
    int     stock_on_hand;
    int     reorder_level;
};
```

Defining an instance of a structure

The structure declaration above is not a definition – no memory space is allocated for the data objects specified. All that exists after the declaration is the new, programmer-defined, data type **struct stock_type**. This is a grouping of data declarations that may be used to define structure variables. To define a structure variable with a *variable list*, use this form:

```
struct stock_type
{
    char    item_name[30];
    char    part_number[10];
    double  cost_price;
    double  sell_price;
    int     stock_on_hand;
    int     reorder_level;
}stock_item;
```

Now, we have defined an instance of the data type **struct stock_type**, for which memory is allocated and which is called **stock_item**. You can put multiple names in the variable list to define multiple instances of the structure.

There is a better way of defining instances of a structure. For example, the definition:

```
struct stock_type stock_item1;
```

creates an instance of the **stock_type** structure in memory and separates the declaration of the structure from its definition. This method allows the programmer to put the structure declaration in a **#include** file and later to define instances of that declaration in the program.

Structure members

The component data objects of a structure are called *members.* In the **stock_type** example, there are six members of the structure and every instance of the structure has the same six members. To refer to an individual structure member, you use this syntax:

```
stock_item1.cost_price
```

The 'dot' or 'member of' operator references **cost_price** as a member of **stock_item1**, which is defined as an instance of the structure type **struct stock_type**.

There's nothing wrong with defining an array as a member of a structure. You access the fifth element of the array **item_name** like this:

```
stock_item1.item_name[4]
```

A structure may have one or more members which are also structures. A structure must not contain an instance of itself.

It's legal to assign to a structure another structure of identical type. However, you can't compare two structures using the equality operator ==. Each of the structure members must be individually compared.

```
stock_item2 = stock_item1;       // assignment, OK
if (stock_item1 == stock_item2)    // comparison, wrong
```

Nested structures

You can define a structure member that is itself a structure. Here's an example of nested structure declarations and definitions:

```
struct stock_type
{
    char    item_name[30];
    char    part_number[10];
    struct detail
    {
        int   height;
        int   width;
        int   depth;
        struct bin
        {
            char    building[50];
            int               floor;
            int               bay;
            int               shelf;
            int               quantity;
        }bin_loc;
        char        special_reqs[50];
        char        part_number[10];
    }item_detail;
    double  cost_price;
    double  sell_price;
    int       stock_on_hand;
    int       reorder_level;
};
// define an instance of the outermost structure
struct stock_type stock_item;
```

> Writing the instance name between the closing } and the semi-colon, creates an instance of the struct declaration.

The structure **item_detail** is nested within **stock_item** and contains further information about the stock item. The structure **bin_loc** is in turn nested within **item_detail** and holds information about a bin location. In C, it is unusual to nest structures fully in this way. The more typical, and entirely equivalent, syntax is this:

```
struct bin
{
    char    building[50];
    int       floor;
    int       bay;
    int       shelf;
```

```
        int     quantity;
};
struct detail
{
    int     height;
    int     width;
    int     depth;
    struct bin      bin_loc;
    char    special_reqs[50];
    char    part_number[10];
};
struct stock_type
{
    char            item_name[30];
    char            part_number[10];
    struct detail   item_detail;
    double          cost_price;
    double          sell_price;
    int             stock_on_hand;
    int             reorder_level;
};
```

```
struct stock_type stock_item;
```

In either case, you find the height of a particular item with this code:

```
stock_item.item_detail.height
```

and the shelf on which that item is stored is:

```
stock_item.item_detail.bin_loc.shelf
```

In the second form, the three structures are declared and defined in reverse order. You have to do this to conform with C's scope rules. The declaration of **struct detail** is in scope for the definition of **item_detail** because it appears first. If the declaration of **struct detail** were instead to follow that of **struct stock_type**, a compiler error would result, flagging **struct detail** as an unknown type.

You can use the name of a structure member either in other structures or as the identifier for an elementary data object, without any clash. In this example, the identifier **part_number** is unique because it must be suffixed to a structure name by the dot operator:

```
stock_item.part_number
```

Assigning values to a structure instance

This simple program, **initstr1.c**, assigns values to the members of a structure of type **struct stock_type** and displays the contents:

```
/************************************************************************
 *
 *      'initstr1.c' – declares a structure and assigns values to its
 *      members. Then it passes an instance of the structure
 *      to a function that displays the members' values
 *
 ***********************************************************************/
#include <stdio.h>
#include <stdlib.h>   // needed to declare 'atoi' and 'atof'

struct stock_type
{
    char        item_name[30];
    char        part_number[30];
    double      cost_price;
    double      sell_price;
    int         stock_on_hand;
    int         reorder_level;
};

int main(void)
{
    struct stock_type stock_item;
    char   instring[50];

    printf("Enter item name ");
    gets(stock_item.item_name);
    printf("Enter part number ");
    gets(stock_item.part_number);
    printf("Enter cost price ");
    gets(instring);
    stock_item.cost_price = atof(instring);
    printf("Enter sell price ");
    gets(instring);
    stock_item.sell_price = atof(instring);
```

printf statements prompt the user for data. **gets** functions are used to read input directly into character-array members.

For numeric members, the user's input is stored in a character array instring before being converted by **atoi** or **atof** to its numeric form.

```
        printf("Enter stock on hand ");
        gets(instring);
        stock_item.stock_on_hand = atoi(instring);
        printf("Enter reorder level ");
        gets(instring);
        stock_item.reorder_level = atoi(instring);

        printf("%s\n", stock_item.item_name);
        printf("%s\n", stock_item.part_number);
        printf("%f\n", stock_item.cost_price);
        printf("%f\n", stock_item.sell_price);
        printf("%d\n", stock_item.stock_on_hand);
        printf("%d\n", stock_item.reorder_level);

        return(0);
}
```

A series of **printf**s is used to display the contents of the structure members.

The **main** function first defines an instance of the structure type **struct stock_type**:

```
struct stock_type stock_item;
```

Defining an array of structures

You can define arrays of structures in the same way as arrays of any other data object. Look at the structure **struct bin**:

```
struct bin
{
    char    building[50];
    int     floor;
    int     bay;
    int     shelf;
    int     quantity;
};
```

There are probably many bin locations where a given item is stored, perhaps dispersed among different buildings. Each bin location might be numbered up to a maximum. You can hold all the bin location detail in an array of structures of type **struct bin**:

```
struct bin bin_arr[20];
```

Now you can search for a bin which has one of the items in stock:

```
int i;

for (i=0; i < 20; i++)
{
    if (bin_arr[i].quantity != 0)
    {
        // Item found
        printf ("bay %d shelf %d in building %s ",
            bin_arr[i].bay,
            bin_arr[i].shelf,
            bin_arr[i].building);

        // Take one out of stock
        bin_arr[i].quantity -= 1;
        break;
    }
}
```

Initialising a structure instance

You will remember that initialisation of a variable happens at the point of its definition, while assignment takes place sometime after the definition. The program **initstr1.c** makes assignments to a structure instance. Now we're going to see how to initialise one. In fact, initialising a structure is like initialising an array.

Using the familiar declaration and definition of **stock_type** and **stock_item**, here is how **stock_item** is initialised:

```
struct stock_type
{
    char    item_name[30];
    char    part_number[10];
    double  cost_price;
    double  sell_price;
    int     stock_on_hand;
    int     reorder_level;
};
```

```
struct stock_type stock_item =
{
    "Turbocharged sewing machine",
    "8705145B",
    275.65,
    340.00,
    50,
    20
};
```

All the initialising expressions should be of the same types as the corresponding structure members, otherwise compile-time errors may result. Similarly, the initialising string constants should be shorter than the sizes of the array members of the structure to allow inclusion of the null character as terminator.

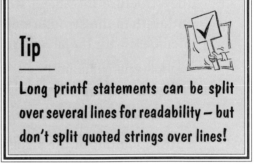

Tip

Long printf statements can be split over several lines for readability — but don't split quoted strings over lines!

Pointers to structures

Pointers to structure members

You can define a structure and a structure pointer like this:

```
struct stock_type
{
    char    item_name[30];
    char    part_number[10];
    double  cost_price;
    double  sell_price;
    int     stock_on_hand;
    int     reorder_level;
};

struct stock_type stock_item;
struct stock_type *sptr = &stock_item;
```

Notice that **sptr**, the structure pointer, is initialised to the address of the structure instance, **stock_item**. You can use the pointer **sptr** rather than the structure name **stock_item** to access the structure's members with the arrow operator:

```
sptr->part_number
```

```
sptr->part_number[5]
```

```
sptr->stock_on_hand
```

sptr is pointing at the structure instance and that the 'object at' **sptr** (***sptr**) is the structure data itself. Therefore, the syntax **sptr->*member*** is equivalent to **(*sptr).*member***.

Pointers to structure instances

Pointers to structures are used for two main purposes. First, they are used to pass structures as arguments between functions. Structures are often very large, with a large amount of memory allocated to them. There is a significant overhead in copying large structures as arguments between functions, especially if the called functions are heavily used. Second, pointers to structures are used for the construction of linked lists, which I refer to in *Linked structures* in Chapter 7.

The program **initstr2.c** illustrates use of pointers to structures as arguments.

pointers to structures

```c
/***********************************************************************
 *
 *      'initstr2.c' – declares a structure and assigns values  to its
 *      members. Then it passes a pointer to an instance of the
 *      structure to a function displays which the members' values
 *
 ***********************************************************************/
#include <stdio.h>
#include <stdlib.h>

struct stock_type
{
    char    item_name[30];
    char    part_number[30];
    double  cost_price;
    double  sell_price;
    int     stock_on_hand;
    int     reorder_level;
};

void disp_stock(struct stock_type *);

int main(void)
{
    struct stock_type stock_item;
    char    instring[50];

    printf("Enter item name ");
    gets(stock_item.item_name);
    printf("Enter part number ");
    gets(stock_item.part_number);
    printf("Enter cost price ");
    gets(instring);
    stock_item.cost_price = atof(instring);
```

```
        printf("Enter sell price ");
        gets(instring);
        stock_item.sell_price = atof(instring);
        printf("Enter stock on hand ");
        gets(instring);
        stock_item.stock_on_hand = atoi(instring);
        printf("Enter reorder level ");
        gets(instring);
        stock_item.reorder_level = atoi(instring);
        disp_stock(&stock_item);

        return(0);
}

void disp_stock(struct stock_type *sptr)
{
        printf("%s\n", sptr->item_name);
        printf("%s\n", sptr->part_number);
        printf("%f\n", sptr->cost_price);
        printf("%f\n", sptr->sell_price);
        printf("%d\n", sptr->stock_on_hand);
        printf("%d\n", sptr->reorder_level);
}
```

> The address of **stock_item** is passed to the function through the pointer **sptr**.

This is functionally equivalent to **initstr1.c**. The difference is that the address of the structure **stock_item** is passed as an argument to the function **disp_stock** and the parameter **sptr** is then used as a pointer to refer to the structure members for display.

You don't have to use pointers when passing structures as parameters; it's possible instead to copy the whole structure instance. Here is the code that does it:

```
// Pass the structure instance to 'disp_stock'
    disp_stock(stock_item);
}

void disp_stock(struct stock_type sitem)
{
    printf("%s",sitem.item_name);
    printf("%s",sitem.part_number);
```

```
        printf("%f",sitem.cost_price);
        printf("%f",sitem.sell_price);
        printf("%d",sitem.stock_on_hand);
        printf("%d",sitem.reorder_level);
}
```

The code has been rewritten so that the instance of the structure, stock_item, is copied in a call by value to the function **disp_stock**. The data is copied into the parameter **sitem**, which is then used in the ordinary way, referencing its members using the dot operator.

Here is what the program displayed when I executed it:

```
Enter item name B747 Engine
Enter part number 74756001
Enter cost price 2500000.01
Enter sell price 3000000.01
Enter stock on hand 30
Enter reorder level 10
B747 Engine
74756001
2500000.010000
3000000.010000
30
10
```

It is almost always more efficient to pass large data objects, such as arrays and structures, as arguments between functions, using their addresses, rather than copying the whole structure. Copying structures between functions can result in significant overhead as member data of the structure is repeatedly pushed and popped in the system's stack space, which is used for transfer of arguments.

Exercises

1. Write a program, **scopy.c**, (without use of the library functions) that copies the contents of one string to another and displays the result.

2. Now write a cleverer program, **mincopy.c**, (without use of the library functions) that uses the minimum amount of code necessary to do the work of **scopy.c**. (I give prizes for the shortest version of this program, so let me know if you think you've got a winner. The current champion has one (only) line of code in main).

3. Write a program that accepts an input string. The contents of the string should be a sequence of characters in the range 0 – 9. There should be no more than six such characters. Validate the string as being an integer in the range 0 – 999999. Convert it to integer and display it. Use the library functions here if you need them.

4. Write a program that accepts an input string and then displays it with the characters in reverse order.

7 Pointers

Linked structures

One of the major uses of pointers is in allowing construction of advanced data structures such as linked lists. Linked lists are built from structure instances, connected by pointers. A structure must not contain a nested instance of itself, but it may contain a pointer to one of its own kind. This allows us to build chains of structure instances that are, in fact, lists.

The following paragraphs gently introduce the mechanisms used in manipulation of linked lists. I use a pair of structure instances, defined in the conventional (non-dynamic) manner. These contain pointers of their own type, allowing one to be linked to the other by containing its address. The address link is used to traverse the simple two-element list. (Coverage of dynamic memory allocation is deferred to page 122.)

Here is an example of a structure declaration containing a pointer to another structure of the same type:

```
struct node
{
    int    x;
    double y;
    struct node *next;
};
```

next is a pointer to a data object of type **struct node**. Let's define two instances of this structure:

```
struct node first, second;
```

Take note

This chapter introduces some of the more advanced pointer syntax and techniques. It does not give a comprehensive coverage of these, particularly the fearsome dark corners of pointers to functions, double pointer indirection and advanced data structures. If you feel a real need to get into the hairy syntax and techniques of C, you might like to try another of my books, the *Newnes C Pocket Book* (2edn), ISBN 0-7506-2538-4.

We assign values to the structure members like this:

```
first.x    = 5;
first.y    = 34.78;
second.x   = 6;
second.y   = 45.89;
```

and now link the structures by assigning the address of the second to the pointer member of the first:

```
first.next = &second;
```

After the address assignment, next is the address of the second structure and the structures' members can be accessed like this:

```
first.x          // 5
first.y          // 34.78
second.x         // 6
second.y         // 45.89
first.next->x    // 6
first.next->y    // 45.89
second.next      // indeterminate value, should be set to NULL.
```

If we define and initialise a pointer to a structure of type **struct node**:

```
struct node *tptr = &first;
```

Now the members of the two structures can be accessed using the pointer notation:

```
tptr->x          // 5
tptr->y          // 34.78
tptr->next->x    // 6
tptr->next->y    // 45.89
```

The list's organisation can be depicted graphically:

sizeof operator

You can use the **sizeof** operator when you need to know the size in bytes or characters in memory occupied by a data object.

In nearly all C environments, a **char** occupies the same amount of memory as an 8-bit byte, but the equivalence is machine-dependent and there are cases where this is not so. The sizes of other data objects – **float**, **int** and so on – are machine-dependent and no assumptions should be made about them when writing portable code.

In most cases, you don't want to know the actual number of bytes occupied by a particular data object. The object occupies a certain amount of space. You need to be able to access that value (without necessarily knowing what it is) so that you can use it later in your program.

The **sizeof** operator returns the size in bytes of its operand. If the operand is a type-specifier, it must be enclosed in parentheses; if it is a variable, the parentheses are optional. **sizeof** is used like this:

```
sizeof variable name;
sizeof (type specifier);
```

Examples of **sizeof** in use with typical data declarations and definitions:

```
char      c;
int       i;
double    d;
float     f;
char      carr[10];
int       iarr[5];
char      *cptr;
int       *iptr = iarr;

sizeof(c)       // 1 by definition
sizeof(i)       // 4 if 32-bit system
sizeof(d)       // 8 if 32-bit system
sizeof(f)       // 4 if 32-bit system
sizeof(carr)    // 10: note the exception!
sizeof(iarr)    // 20 if 32-bit system
sizeof(cptr)    // 2 or 4
sizeof(iptr)    // 4 if 32-bit system
```

```
// type sizes
sizeof(int)         // 4 if 32-bit system
sizeof(char)        // 1 by definition
sizeof(float)       // 4 if 32-bit system
sizeof(double)      // 8 if 32-bit system
```

Suppose that we declare a simple structure:

```
struct sp_cell_s
{
    int     ival;
    double  dval;
    char    sval[20];
};
```

The value of **sizeof(struct sp_cell_s)** is at least 32, assuming a 4-byte integer, an 8-byte double and adding the 20-byte array, plus the total of bytes, if any, needed for member alignment.

sizeof is special in that it is a *compile-time operator* which yields a constant value. **sizeof** therefore can only yield information that is available to the compiler. It cannot know, for example, what the contents of a pointer will be at some point during program execution; it can only report the size of the pointer itself, not what it may in the future point to.

If the operand of **sizeof** is an array name, the extent of the memory occupied by the array is available at compile time thanks to specification of a constant-expression subscript limit. In this case, as an exception (see **carr** above), the array name is treated not as the address of the array but as representing the actual memory occupied by the array.

Programmer-defined data types

So far, you have seen four storage class specifiers: **auto**, **extern**, **static**, **register**. There is a fifth, **typedef**, which allows you to define original data types of arbitrary complexity. **typedef** fits uneasily as a member of C's storage class specifiers. It is really a method by which you can define new type specifiers in terms of existing types. It is also a useful shorthand. Type definitions made using **typedef** are usually grouped in header files and used in program as type specifiers like any other.

Let's look (again!) at the structure declaration **struct stock_type**:

```
struct stock_type
{
    char    item_name[30];
    char    part_number[10];
    double  cost_price;
    double  sell_price;
    int     stock_on_hand;
    int     reorder_level;
};
```

Assume that all prices are stored as double floating-point numbers. We can then make the following type definition:

```
typedef double price;
```

and define instances of the new type:

```
price   cost_price;
price   sell_price;
```

More complex type definitions

The example above serves no purpose other than, perhaps, to improve program readability. We are interested in more complex definitions.

```
typedef struct stock_type
{
    char    item_name[30];
    char    part_number[10];
    double  cost_price;
    double  sell_price;
    int     stock_on_hand;
    int     reorder_level;
}ITEM;
```

In this case, **ITEM** is not a definition of an instance of the structure type **struct stock_type** but is instead a *synonym* for the data type **struct stock_type**. Now we can define instances of the structure using:

    ITEM item1, item2;

Using the self-referencing structure declaration given on page 110:

```
typedef struct node
{
    int    x;
    double  y;
    struct node *next;
}NODE;
```

NODE is now a data type specifying the structure type **struct node**. To define two of these structures and a structure pointer, we make the definitions and initialisation:

    NODE first, second, *tptr = &first;

tptr may now be used as earlier (page 111) to reference the members of the two structures.

Specification of new types based on structures is very common. It is typical to provide a type definition for both a structure instance and a pointer of the structure's type:

```
typedef struct node
{
    int    x;
    doubley;
    struct node *next;
}NODE, *PNODE;
```

Once these types have been defined and incorporated in a header file, you can use pointers of the structure's type without having to be concerned with the asterisk pointer notation:

    NODE inst;
    PNODE nptr = &inst;

The array type

A complex use of **typedef** that is often not understood is this:

    typedef char array_type[256];

Here, **array_type** is *not* the name of a character array of 256 elements; it is rather a type representing *character-arrays-of-256-elements*. It can be used to define actual arrays of 256 elements:

```
array_type a1_256 = "Three thousand ducats, a good round sum";
```

such that the following statement yields the character 'h':

```
printf("%c\n", a1_256[7]);
```

Preprocessor and typedef compared

Another use of **typedef** that some programmers favour, is this:

```
typedef char *charptr;
```

Now **charptr** is a synonym for **char *** and you can use it to define character pointers:

```
charptr cptr1, cptr2;
```

It is important to understand C's different shorthand mechanisms. For example, use of **typedef** and the preprocessor may give superficially similar results. Here, both **char1** and **char2** are character pointers:

```
#define PCHAR char *
typedef char * charptr;
PCHAR    char1;
charptr    char2;
```

but the next definitions expose the difference between pattern substitution as implemented by the preprocessor and the true type synonym provided by **typedef**:

```
// substitutes to: char *char1, char2;
PCHAR char1, char2;
// correctly defined as char *char1, *char2;
charptr char1, char2;
```

Portability

typedef can be useful in producing portable programs:

```
typedef long INT;
INT portable_int;
```

portable_int is a long integer on both 16- and 32-bit systems. This would ensure that code written for a 32-bit system such as Windows 95 is portable without change to the DOS/Windows 3.X combination.

Dynamic storage allocation

Up to now, the only way we have seen of allocating memory space to a variable is by definition of that variable and allocation of space by the compiler. All variables up to this point have been of fixed length and memory allocation has been outside the programmer's control.

An array of structures is the best way we have so far seen of storing repeated instances of aggregate data. However, arrays are of fixed length, determined at compile time. If the records were being generated from data entered at a device such as a terminal, then no matter how large the array defined to store the data, it might not be large enough.

What is needed is a way of allocating memory, under the control of the programmer, at program run time. This is done using four functions, the prototypes of which are in the standard header file **stdlib.h**:

malloc   returns a pointer to a specified amount of memory, allocated from the program heap by the C dynamic allocation system.

calloc   does the same as malloc, but returns a pointer to an array of allocated memory and initialises that memory with zeros.

realloc   changes the extent of memory allocated by **malloc** or **calloc** and associated with a pointer, while preserving the contents.

free   frees allocated memory and makes it available to the heap.

Of these functions, you only need **malloc** and **free** to write programs which use dynamic allocation and it is these we shall concentrate on.

Dynamic storage allocation must be used in any situation in which you don't know in advance how much data will be entered to a program. Such an eventuality usually takes either of two forms:

●   data records are entered by an operator; the receiving program uses dynamic allocation of a structure for each unit of record data entered to create a list or file of effectively unlimited length.

●   a text string entered by an operator is stored in an input buffer of the maximum possible line length (say 512 characters). To record each line in a page of text as 512 characters wastes memory, so dynamic allocation is used to point each line's pointer to just enough memory to hold the actual text and the null-terminator.

Later in this section, I'll show you how to use dynamic allocation to implement the linked structures shown earlier. (For a full-blown linked list done with dynamic allocation, see the *Newnes C Pocket Book*.) But first, let's explore the operation of **malloc** and **free**.

Calling malloc

Let's look again at the structure declaration:

```
typedef struct node
{
    int     x;
    double  y;
    struct node *next;
}NODE;
```

Recall that **NODE** is not a structure definition but a **typedef** giving a new type specifier representing a structure of type **struct node**.

Let's now allocate enough space for such a structure. To do this , we need to know its size, and we find this using the **sizeof** operator:

```
sizeof(NODE) // returns structure size in bytes
```

malloc takes one parameter, the size in bytes of the object for which memory is to be allocated. Memory for one instance of the structure is allocated like this:

```
malloc(sizeof(NODE))
```

malloc returns a pointer to the memory if the memory is successfully allocated, otherwise NULL. Assign the **malloc** return value to a pointer of the same type as the data object for which space is being allocated:

```
NODE *ptr1;
ptr1 = ((NODE *)malloc(sizeof(NODE)))
```

The result of the **malloc** call is assigned to the pointer **ptr1**, a pointer to a structure of type **NODE**. **malloc**, however, returns a pointer of type **void**. Here, the return value of **malloc** is typecast with **NODE *** (pointer to **NODE**) and assigned to **ptr1**.

After a successful call to **malloc**, **ptr1** points to an instance in memory of structure type **NODE,** otherwise **ptr1** holds **NULL**. This leads us to the complete construct for allocation of memory:

```
if ((ptr1 = ((NODE *)malloc(sizeof(NODE)))) == NULL)
{
    printf("Memory allocation error\n");
    exit(0);          // Exit program
}
// Memory successfully allocated
```

The prototype for the **exit** library function is in the header file **stdlib.h**. It causes graceful program termination and returns a status code to the operating system. Zero indicates a successful termination.

In general, you can use the combination of **malloc** and **sizeof** to allocate memory dynamically (at run time) for any data object. The operand of **sizeof** may be either an instance of the object for which memory has already been assigned or the object's type specifier.

Freeing allocated memory

The most common serious error made in C programs is that of using a pointer before it has been pointed to an allocated memory object. A second error is failure to release allocated memory when it is no longer required. Failure to free allocated memory is actually more insidious than use of an uninitialised pointer.

If you don't subsequently deallocate dynamically-allocated memory with the function **free**, the memory is not returned to the available pool, even when the program ends. This leads to a situation where the system gradually runs out of memory, often resulting in a program crash far from the point where memory should have been freed. It can be extremely difficult to track down the source of such a *memory leak.*

For every dynamic memory allocation in a program, there should be a corresponding use of **free** to make available its memory. If the pointer **ptr1** is associated with memory allocated by **malloc**, **calloc** or **realloc**, that memory is deallocated by the function call:

```
free(ptr1);
```

Memory deallocation is usually done when that memory is no longer needed, for example when a list element or line of text is deleted.

Dynamic allocation of list nodes

Now we know enough to do a second version of the linked structures shown earlier. There, the two instances of NODE are allocated with a conventional definition:

```
struct node first, second;
```

With dynamic allocation, the space is reserved using this code:

```
NODE *tptr1, *tptr2;
if ((tptr1 = ((NODE *)malloc(sizeof(NODE)))) == NULL)
{
    printf("Memory error allocating first node\n");
    exit(0);// Exit program
}
if ((tptr2 = ((NODE *)malloc(sizeof(NODE)))) == NULL)
{
    printf("Memory error allocating second node\n");
    exit(0);// Exit program
}
```

Now we can make the assignments of values to the structure instances' members:

```
tptr1->next = tptr2;       // Link the two structures

tptr1->x   = 5;
tptr1->y   = 34.78;
tptr2->x   = 6;
tptr2->y   = 45.89;
tptr2->next = NULL;
```

In a real implementation of a list program, the dynamic allocation code and the assignments would be in a loop controlled by the user's input. In addition, you would have to manage the links between the list's members as well as strategies for insertion in and deletion from the list.

When there is no more use for the allocated nodes, you should take care to return to the free list the memory allocated for them:

```
free(tptr1);
free(tptr2);
```

Address arithmetic

You can do address arithmetic on pointers, usually with pointers to arrays. You've already seen many typical cases of address arithmetic: where the displacement of a character pointer from its start point needs to be calculated in order to return a relative position in a string. Also, you should have become used to the practice of repeatedly incrementing pointer values by one when traversing an array.

Let **ptr** be a pointer to an array of elements of some type.

ptr++ increments the pointer to the next element in the array.

***ptr** is the content of the element currently pointed to.

ptr += n increments the pointer by the value of **n** array elements.

Each element of a character array is, by definition, one **char** long. It is reasonable to expect a pointer to such an array to be incremented by one to point to the next element. In fact, for all arrays of any type, the 'increment by one' rule holds. The size of each element is taken into account and it is a mistake, when incrementing the array pointer, to try to calculate the size of the array elements and increment by that amount. *Incrementing a pointer by one makes it point to the next element for all arrays, regardless of the type of the elements.*

Address arithmetic example

Look again at the structure declaration **struct stock_type**:

```
struct stock_type
{
    char    item_name[30];
    char    part_number[10];
    double  cost_price;
    double  sell_price;
    int     stock_on_hand;
    int     reorder_level;
};
```

Now we define an array of these structures and initialise a pointer to the array:

```
struct stock_type stockarr[100];
struct stock_type *stockptr = stockarr;
int  count;
```

Even though each array element occupies at least 50 bytes, the pointer need only be repeatedly incremented by one to traverse the array:

```
for (count = 0; count < 100; count++,stockptr++)
{
    // Set the array elements zero or empty
    stockptr->item_name[0]   = '\0';
    ...
    stockptr->reorder_level  = 0;
}
```

When two pointers to an array are subtracted, the result is not the number of bytes that separate the array elements but the number of array elements.

Take note

Do not do arithmetic of this kind on pointers of different types; the results may be catastrophic. Two pointers of the same type may be subtracted but *not added, divided or multiplied*. Addition to a pointer is only legal where the pointer is incremented by an integral (small whole-number) value.

Precedence and associativity

You need to be careful with the syntax of pointer increment and decrement operations. The ++, -- and * (dereferencing) operators are all of the same precedence and associate right-to-left. As a result, some unexpected things can happen when these operators are mixed in the same expression. For example, ***ptr++** is a very common expression. It means that the object at **ptr** is fetched (first) and then (second) the *pointer value* is incremented by one. If we want to add one to the *object at the pointer*, we need **(*ptr)++**.

Liberal use of parentheses in the case of mixed-operator expressions like that above and care about not mixing pointer types will save a lot of trouble. The program **ptrinc.c** illustrates the point.

```
/**********************************************************************
*
*        'ptrinc.c' — Program to illustrate compound pointer arithmetic
*
**********************************************************************/
#include <stdio.h>

char stg[] = "nmlkjihgfedcba";

int main(void)
{
    char *ptr = stg;

    printf("Initial string is %s\n\n",ptr);
    printf("Display and post-increment the pointer\n");
    printf("*ptr++ %c\n",*ptr++);
    printf("*ptr %c\n\n",*ptr);

    printf("Re-initialise pointer\n");
    ptr = stg;
    printf("Display and post-increment the OBJECT AT the pointer\n");
    printf("(*ptr)++ %c\n",(*ptr)++);
    printf("*ptr %c\n",*ptr);

    return(0);

}
```

> ***ptr++** retrieves data and increments the pointer **ptr**

> **(*ptr)++** adds 1 to the data ('n'), giving 'o'

When you run the program, you get this screen display:

```
Initial string is nmlkjihgfedcba

Display and post-increment the pointer
*ptr++ n
*ptr m

Re-initialise pointer
Display and post-increment the OBJECT AT the pointer
(*ptr)++ n
*ptr o
```

*ptr++ is probably one of the most common forms of expression used in all C programming so, again, don't get the idea that this pointer-arithmetic stuff is for nerds. It's part of everyday C programming, can become very complex, and you need to be adept at it.

Arrays of pointers

In C, you can define a pointer to a pointer (or a pointer to a pointer to a pointer if you like). Pointers to pointers are sometimes called *multiply-indirected* pointers. An important application of multiply-indirected pointers is in accessing and traversing pointer arrays. Implementing an N-dimensional array in C using pointers requires definition of a pointer array of N-1 dimensions. In the case of a two-dimensional character array, which can store a page of text, we must define a one-dimensional array of pointers of type **char ***.

```
char *cptr[10];
```

Each of the pointers in the array must be initialised to the address of an array of characters before being used:

```
char *cptr[10] = {"Signor Antonio, many a time and oft\n",
    "on the Rialto, you have rated me\n",
    "for my moneys and my usances.\n",
    "Still have I borne it with a patient shrug,",
    "for sufferance is the badge of all our tribe.", ""};
```

Here, pointers 0 to 4 of the ten-element pointer array are initialised to the addresses of the five literal strings shown within curly braces.

cptr[1] points to the string *"on the Rialto, you have rated me\n"*. Instead of using subscripts to access array elements, we can use a pointer to the array of pointers:

```
char **cpp = cptr;
```

After the pointer initialisation:

- ***cpp** points to the string *"Signor Antonio, many a time and oft\n"*.
- ****cpp** is the first character in that string, 'S'.
- **(*cpp)++** increments the pointer to the first string; ****cpp** is now the second character, 'i'.

Program example: array2d.c

Here is an example program that exercises many of the possible operations using a pointer to pointers on an array of pointers to strings. The array of pointers is defined and initialised to its six component strings outside **main**.

124

The program performs two principal operations. The first displays each of the text lines with subscripts; the second does the same with pointers.

You should inspect this program carefully and understand it because the methods of single and double indirection shown here are generally applicable for all cases in C where arrays of pointers are used.

```c
/*********************************************************************
 *
 *      'array2d.c' – Program to initialise a two-dimensional
 *                    character array and display its contents
 *
 *********************************************************************/
#include <stdio.h>

char *cptr[] = {"Signor Antonio, many a time and oft\n",
                "on the Rialto, you have rated me\n",
                "for my moneys and my usances.\n",
                "Still have I borne it with a patient shrug,\n",
                "for sufferance is the badge of all our tribe.",""};

int main(void)
{
    char **cpp;      // Pointer to array of pointers
    char ans[5];
    int i;

    // Display all the strings using subscripts
    printf("\nPress RETURN to continue ");
    gets(ans);

    for (i = 0; *cptr[i] != NULL; i++)
        printf("%s",cptr[i]);

    // Now do the same, with pointers
    printf("\nPress RETURN to continue ");
    gets(ans);

    for (cpp = cptr; **cpp != NULL; cpp++)
        printf("%s",*cpp);

    return(0);
}
```

The iteration is terminated when the first character of a string pointed at by one of the array of pointers is '\0'.

The output of array2d.c is this:

```
Press RETURN to continue
Signor Antonio, many a time and oft
on the Rialto, you have rated me
for my moneys and my usances.
Still have I borne it with a patient shrug,
for sufferance is the badge of all our tribe.
Press RETURN to continue
Signor Antonio, many a time and oft
on the Rialto, you have rated me
for my moneys and my usances.
Still have I borne it with a patient shrug,
for sufferance is the badge of all our tribe.
```

Command-line arguments

In all examples presented in earlier chapters, you have entered data via such functions as **gets** and **scanf**. The **main** function has never been supplied with arguments.

You can make the **main** function to take parameters so that the user can enter a command at the shell level of the operating system. The DOS and OS/2 copy command:

    C:\> copy file1 file2

shows a C program in operation. You are not prompted for the file names. As you would expect, you enter them on the command line.

To set up command-line arguments in your C program, you use the special arguments **argc** and **argv** in the **main** function header. The **main** function header with command-line arguments looks like this:

    int main(int argc, char *argv[])

argc is an integer value that holds the number of arguments on the command line. Its minimum value is 1, as the program name qualifies as an argument. In the copy example above, the value of **argc** is 3.

argv is a pointer to an array of character pointers. Each of the character pointers in the array points to a string. Each of the strings is a single command line argument.

Again considering the copy example:

argv[0]	points to	"copy"
argv[1]	points to	"file1"
argv[2]	points to	"file2"

argv[argc] is always a null pointer. In the copy example, **argc** has the value 3, which is 1 more than the number of arguments, counting from 0.

The empty brackets **[]** of **argv** indicate that it is an array of undetermined length. Its actual length is established at runtime, when it is initialised with the command-line arguments entered by the user.

You could also write the main header as:

```
int main (int argc, char **argv)
```

In the program code, ***argv** could be used in place of **argv[0]**, ***++argv** in place of **argv[1]**, ***++argv** instead of **argv[2]**, and so on.

In this case, keeping track of pointers is less convenient than using subscripts, which is why double indirection on command-line arguments is often not used.

There follows a minimal example of a complete program, **cmdarg.c**, that uses command-line arguments. It doesn't do anything other than accept the command line and, using various techniques, display the individual arguments. Here it is:

```
/**********************************************************************
 *
 *      'cmdarg.c' – use of command-line arguments.
 *
 **********************************************************************/
#include <stdio.h>
#include <stdlib.h>

int main(int argc, char *argv[])
{
    FILE *inp, *outp;
    char **argvp = argv + 1;
```

Define pointer and initialise to point to first argument after the name.

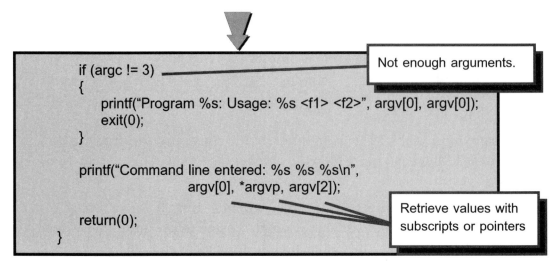

```
        if (argc != 3)                                    Not enough arguments.
        {
            printf("Program %s: Usage: %s <f1> <f2>", argv[0], argv[0]);
            exit(0);
        }

        printf("Command line entered: %s %s %s\n",
                            argv[0], *argvp, argv[2]);      Retrieve values with
                                                           subscripts or pointers
        return(0);
    }
```

cmdarg.c expects a command-line something like this:

    cmdarg argtext1 argtext2

There must be three arguments in total, including the program's name. Otherwise, the 'Usage' message is displayed and program execution stops with the **exit** library function call. Assuming that three arguments are specified, then all three are displayed by the **printf** that follows.

The program name and the third argument (argtext2) are displayed using subscripted references to **argv**. The program displays the first argument (argtext1) using a doubly-indirected pointer. **argvp** is a pointer-to-pointer initialised to be the same as the argument pointer **argv**. If **argvp** is the same as **argv** and therefore points to the string "cmdarg", then **argvp + 1** points to the string "argtext1".

If you run the program without arguments, the screen display will be similar to this:

    Program C:\CMDARG.EXE: Usage: C:\CMDARG.EXE <f1> <f2>

With the proper number of arguments, you get the following:

    Command line entered: C:\CMDARG.EXE argtext1 argtext2

Pointers to functions

Use of pointers to functions is one of the aspects of C syntax that most intimidates novice (and not-so-novice!) C programmers. In fact, function pointers are no more than a logical completion of the general pointer syntax.

Functions are not variables, but you can define pointers to them, store such pointers in arrays and pass them as arguments between functions.

Function pointers are typically used in specific classes of application:

- where a function's identity is to be supplied as an argument to another function

- where outside events determine which of many functions is to be called next. In such cases an array of pointers to functions is often used to control function calls.

A pointer to a function contains the internal memory address of the entry point of that function. The address of the function is obtained using only the function's name.

Here is how to define a pointer to a function:

```
int (*fptr)();
```

fptr is a pointer to a function returning an **int**. Note that all the parentheses here are necessary. For example:

```
int *fptr();
```

is not a pointer to a function, but the declaration of a function returning a pointer to an **int**.

Simple example of a function pointer

The program **drawline.c** demonstrates using pointers to functions.

Use of the function pointer is not necessary; you could as easily call the function **drawline** explicitly. **fptr** is defined as a function pointer. The name of the function, **drawline**, is the address of that function. It is assigned to **fptr**, which is then called as a function name exactly as **drawline** could be.

pointers to functions

```c
#include <stdio.h>

void drawline(int);

int main(void)
{
    //    Define a pointer to a function with
    //    an 'int' as a parameter

    void (*fptr)(int len);

    //    Assign a function address to the pointer

    fptr = drawline;

    //    (*fptr)(50); is OK for the function call also
    fptr(50);
    return(0);
}

void drawline(int len)
{
    while (len > 0)
    {
        printf("-");
        len--;
    }
    printf("\n");
}
```

The program draws a horizontal line at the bottom of the screen:

```
--------------------------------------------------------------------------------
```

During function pointer assignment, ISO C also allows the **&** operator to be applied to a function name:

```
fptr    =    drawline;
fptr    =    &drawline;
```

These are equivalent and give the same result.

The function call using the pointer may alternatively be made with dereferencing:

```
(*fptr)(50);
```

Use in real C programs of function pointers is usually much more complex than this. However, the function pointer syntax of **drawline.c** is the basis of all usages of pointers to functions. In this *Made Simple* text, I'm not going to present further examples of programs using function pointers. If you want to find out more, I would again advise you to refer to the *Newnes C Pocket Book*.

Exercises

1. Verify the difference in operation of the preprocessor, as compared with the **typedef** mechanism, described on page 116, '*Preprocessor and typedef compared*'.

2. Modify the program **maxint.c** from Chapter 2 (page 26) so that it uses a **typedef**-defined type **INT**:

   typedef long INT;

   to ensure that the maximum **INT** value is at least 2147483647.

3. Write a program, **lnstruct.c**, that implements the linked-nodes program, described at the start of this chapter.

4. Write a program, **dynstruc.c**, that implements the linked-nodes program, described on page 118, using dynamic memory allocation.

8 The standard C Library

Introduction

The C programming language doesn't include built-in functions for such things as reading and writing files, performing special mathematical functions, performing string manipulation, and doing terminal I/O. Thus, equivalents to the file READ and WRITE of COBOL, the mathematical functions ABS and SQR of Pascal, and the terminal output sequence PUT SKIP of PL/1 are missing from C.

Functions that provide these 'features' are defined, separately, in the standard library. The functions are stored in the library in their compiled, or object-code, form. They are linked (or loaded, depending on your preferred terminology) with the user's program at the link step, after compilation. The output of the load step is an executable program.

Functions, data objects and macros used in the C library are declared in standard header files, listed below. These should be included in the source code of any program that uses C library functions.

Because a large number of standard functions are excluded from the C language definition, the C language itself is small and compilers for it are simpler than for other languages. Only the header files containing references to the functions actually needed are included in a C program; this tends to reduce the size of executable programs.

You're encouraged to use the available functions as building blocks in the construction of complex programs. Any special functions you may develop can become part of your own library or header file and reused in many programs.

You can find the techniques for building libraries as well as the full range of available standard header files in the C compiler documentation for your particular environment. In this chapter, I present a subset of header files and functions that are part of the ISO C standard.

The header files most commonly used are:

stdio.h	standard I/O
string.h	string functions

ctype.h   character class tests

math.h   mathematical functions

stdlib.h   other standard functions

Chapter 9 lists the functions declared in these five header files.

Other standard header files are:

assert.h   diagnostics functions

time.h   time and date functions

stdarg.h   variable argument functions

signal.h   signal/interrupt functions

setjmp.h   function control

limits.h   implementation limits

float.h   magnitude limits

stddef.h   common definitions

errno.h   errors

locale.h   localisation

Standard I/O

The standard I/O header file **stdio.h** contains declarations of functions, defined in the C Library, that handle transfer of data to and from external devices. **stdio.h** provides a standard interface to these devices. Using the library functions, you don't have to rely on operating system-dependent I/O procedures.

Standard I/O files

stdio.h declares pointers to three standard files, which are available, open, to every C program when it starts executing:

```
stdin     standard input
stdout    standard output
stderr    standard error
```

All files are connected to *streams* and the terms file and stream are often used interchangeably.

stdin usually means the terminal input device and may be thought of as representing the keyboard.

stdout usually means the terminal output device and may be thought of as representing the screen.

Output to **stderr** is directed to the standard output device, even if **stdout** is redirected elsewhere.

Standard I/O functions

The library function **getchar** uses standard input to fetch a character of data and assign the data to a variable. **putchar** similarly uses standard output to write a character to the standard output device.

Two additional functions, **getc** and **putc**, are supplied in **stdio.h**. These are more general cases of **getchar** and **putchar**.

```
getc(stdin)       is equivalent to   getchar()
putc(c,stdout)    is equivalent to   putchar(c)
```

As you will see later in this chapter, **getc** and **putc** may be used to do input/output on files other than the standard input and standard output.

stdio.h provides functions for formatted console input/output. We've already seen **printf**, used for output to the standard output device. Up to now, for string input, we have used the function **gets**; the input counterpart of **printf**, which performs similar functions to **gets**, is **scanf**.

stdio.h definitions

stdio.h also contains definitions for the symbolic constants

EOF	end of file
NULL	null character
FILE	file pointer declarator
BUFSIZ	file I-O buffer size

FILE is defined in **stdio.h** as a structure type, using **typedef**. The structure pointed to by a file pointer (of type **FILE ***) holds all the information necessary to control file access, including a pointer which keeps track of the read/write position in the file. The file pointer is used to access a file by all the file **open**, **close**, **read** and **write** functions.

stdin, **stdout** and **stderr** are examples of special file pointers.

Take note

There is a full annotated list of stdio.h functions in Chapter 9.

Formatted I/O functions

The formatted output and input functions, **printf** and **scanf**, are declared in **stdio.h**. They are so heavily used and have so many syntax options that they deserve to be treated separately. Here are their function prototypes:

```
int printf(const char *<format>, ...);
int scanf(const char *<format>, ...);
```

There are also a number of variants of both functions: **fprintf** for formatted output to file; **sprintf** for formatted output to strings; **fscanf** and **sscanf** for formatted input from files and strings.

Up to now, in place of **scanf**, we have used **gets** to read text from the standard input. **scanf** and **printf** are big, powerful functions with many options. For simple text input, **gets** may be more efficient than **scanf**. For simple text output, **puts** may be more efficient than **printf**. Often, however, you need the additional capabilities of **printf** and **scanf**.

printf

The **printf** function in general has two sets of arguments: the format string and a variable list. The format string contains ordinary characters, which are copied to the standard output, and, optionally, format codes, which are letters prefixed by a '**%**'. For each format code specified in the format string, the variable list must contain a corresponding variable of the data type implied by the format code.

printf returns an integer value that represents the number of characters output. The **printf** format codes (see page 158) permit quite sophisticated text output. This example uses **printf** to display a table of squares and cubes of the numbers from 1 to 19:

```c
#include <stdio.h>
int main(void)
{
    float f;
    for (f=1.0; f < 20.0; f++)
        printf("%6.2f %6.2f %6.2f\n", f,f*f, f*f*f);
    return(0);
}
```

In this case, the format code **%6.2f** causes the corresponding floating-point number to be displayed so that they occupy at least 6 spaces of width, including 2 digits after the decimal point.

scanf

scanf is the input form of **printf**. The format codes used by **scanf** and all variants of both **printf** and **scanf** are superficially similar. There are, however, some important differences:

- **scanf** allows specification of field width but not of precision; the field width is a *maximum*, while for **printf** it is a *minimum* value

- The [] conversion sequence is specific to **scanf**.

- **scanf** does not accept **printf** flag characters (see page 160).

You shouldn't use the format codes for **printf** as a guide to those of **scanf**, or vice-versa. Chapter 9 has a full list of **scanf** format codes.

Like **printf**, **scanf** uses two sets of arguments: a format string and a variable list. It reads from the standard input one or more data objects, performs appropriate conversions on them according to the format string specification, and stores the results at the pointers specified in the variable list. The pointer type should be the same as the type of data object implied by the corresponding format code.

It is not possible to display a prompt as part of the **scanf** format string. If a prompt is required, the **scanf** call should be preceded by a **printf**.

A non-whitespace character in the format string causes **scanf** to read and discard a matching input character. For example:

```
scanf("%d/%d/%d", &dd, &mm, &yy);
```

requires that slashes are entered as part of the date input.

scanf stops reading from standard input when it exhausts its format string or encounters a mismatch between one of its format codes and an input data item. It returns as its value the number of data objects read and successfully converted, or EOF if end-of-file or error occurs before any input conversion.

If there is more input data than is required by an item in the **scanf** variable list, unused data will be used by **scanf** as input to the next item, if any. As an example use of **scanf**, we have already seen the **get_data** function in the program **validate.c**:

```
void get_data(int *pyy, int *pmm, int *pdd)
{
    printf("Enter a date of form dd/mm/yy: ");
    scanf("%d/%d/%d",pdd, pmm, pyy);
}
```

Character-array input, followed by explicit conversion calls to **atoi**, are here replaced by the functionality of **scanf**.

sprintf and other functions

The function **sprintf** is the same as **printf** except that, instead of writing to standard output, it places the output at a memory address specified by a character pointer and terminates the output with a null character. The pointer must be initialised to the address of a character array large enough to take the output of the **sprintf** conversion.

The program above, that uses **printf** to display a table of squares and cubes, could be implemented with **sprintf**:

```
#include <stdio.h>
int main(void)
{
    float f;
    char outstr[100];
    for (f=1.0; f < 20.0; f++)
    {
        sprintf(outstr, "%6.2f %6.2f %6.2f\n", f, f*f, f*f*f);
        printf("%s",outstr);
    }
    return(0);
}
```

sscanf is the same as **scanf** except that it takes its input from a string rather than from standard input. **fprintf** and **fscanf** are the file versions of **printf** and **scanf**; they write to and read from files according to rules which are described in the next section.

File handling

The concept of a file in C has its genesis in the original definition of a file in the UNIX operating system. A file is an unstructured collection of character data and may represent a disk file or a peripheral device.

C assumes that the file has no structure: there is no concept in the language of file records, block sizes or similar structures. Any file structure must be imposed on the raw file by the program logic itself.

A *stream* is the conceptual source or destination of data associated with a physical file. A stream is a consistent interface to the C programmer that is independent of the actual device being accessed. An *open* operation, such as **fopen**, associates a stream with a file by means of the file pointer. Once a file is open, you can exchange information between it and a C program.

The **stdio.h** file-access functions, (see Chapter 9), operate on files via streams. A stream may be thought of as a data object of type

    FILE *

or *file pointer*. Each file has a pointer which records the current position in the file. You use the pointer to open and close the file, to read from and write to it and to perform *random access* using the **fseek** library function.

These are the function prototypes, in **stdio.h**, for **fopen** and **fclose**:

    FILE *fopen(const char *s, const char *mode);
    int fclose(FILE *fp);

Example: copying a file

A simple program, **filecopy.c**, follows. It copies the text contents of one disk file to another. First, two file pointers are defined: **inp** and **outp**. The two character arrays are initialised to the names of the input and output files from data input by the user. The familiar **gets** function is used to initialise these strings.

Next, the program attempts to open both files, the first in read mode ("r"), and the second in write mode ("w"). **fopen** returns an object of type **FILE *** that is used subsequently to access the file opened. If either file cannot be opened, the program terminates abnormally.

If the file in read mode cannot be opened, it probably means that the input file is not there to be copied. If the write mode file cannot be opened, it is created. It is unlikely that the program would end abnormally as a result of inability to open a file for output.

file input and output

```
/****************************************************************
*
*       Program filecopy.c — copies an input to an output file
*
****************************************************************/

#include <stdio.h>
#include <stdlib.h>

void filecopy(FILE *, FILE *);

int main(void)
{
    // Define input and output file pointers

    FILE *inp, *outp;
    char   inname[20], outname[20];

    printf("Enter input file name ");
    gets(inname);
    printf("Enter output file name ");
    gets(outname);

    if ((inp = fopen(inname, "r")) == NULL)
    {
        printf("Cannot open input file\n");
        exit(0);
    }

    if ((outp = fopen(outname, "w")) == NULL)
    {
        printf("Cannot open output file\n");
        exit(0);
    }
```

```
        filecopy(inp, outp);

        fclose(inp);
        fclose(outp);
        return(0);
}

void filecopy(FILE *inp, FILE *outp)
{
        int c;

        while ((c = getc(inp)) != EOF)
            putc(c, outp);
}
```

The function **filecopy** is called with the file pointers **inp** and **outp** as parameters. **filecopy** uses the standard I/O functions **getc** and **putc** to read from the input file, one character at a time, and write to the output file. The reads stop when EOF on the input file is encountered.

Finally, in **main**, the two file pointers are supplied as arguments to the **fclose** library function, which closes the files, disassociates the files from the streams and frees the file pointers. To run this program, you issue a command of the form:

    filecopy

at the command line. Apart from the prompts requesting the names of input and output files, the program displays no output; you know that it has worked if file2 is a copy of file1.

All the library functions used in **filecopy.c** in turn call low-level system-specific functions that do the file operations at a lower level. The standard I/O functions ensure a high-level, system-independent interface to files on any system.

It may seem surprising that **getc** and **putc** are used to read and write data on a character-by-character basis. More powerful functions, such as **fgets** and **fputs** both perform repeated calls on **getc** and **putc**.

File access modes

You can use these access modes with the **fopen** function:

"r"   Open a text file for reading and position the read/write pointer at the beginning of the file.

"w"   Open a text file for writing; if it does not already exist, create it; if it does exist, delete it.

"a"   Append to a text file; position the read/write pointer at the end of the file; if the file does not already exist, create it.

"r+"   Open a text file for reading and writing; otherwise same as "r".

"w+"   Open a text file for reading and writing; otherwise same as "w".

"a+"   Append to a text file for reading and writing; otherwise same as "a".

If an access mode is suffixed with "b" in the manner "wb" or "a+b", a binary stream is specified.

Text and binary files

The ISO standard specifies text and binary streams. On some systems, especially UNIX, there is no difference at all between the two.

A text stream is a sequence of lines, terminated by '\n' and containing zero or more characters, which may undergo certain character translations by the local environment. A binary stream undergoes no such translations and, on a given system, will always read the same as it was written. Where binary streams are distinguished from text streams, the behaviour of some standard library functions is altered.

String-based I/O

The **fgets** and **fputs** functions provide a higher-level means of reading from and writing to files than **getc** and **putc**. **fgets** and **fputs** have the following function prototypes:

```
char   *fgets(char *s, int n, FILE *fp);
int fputs(const char *s, FILE *fp);
```

These prototypes are in **stdio.h**. The **fgets** function reads a string from a specified file until either a newline character or a number of characters one less than **s** have been read. The resulting string is null-terminated. Any newline character read is included in the string.

The **fputs** function writes to the output file a null-terminated string pointed to by **s**, followed by a newline. The null character is not copied.

Example – searching a file

A more complex example of a file-processing program, **fsearch.c**, follows. It uses most of the file access functions you've seen so far. The program reads a file line-by-line and searches each line for an occurrence of a specified pattern of characters. The total number of occurrences in the file, if any, is reported.

searching in files

```
/**********************************************************************
*      Program fsearch.c — search for a pattern in a file
**********************************************************************/
#include <stdio.h>
#include <stdlib.h>
#include <string.h>

int strpos(char *, char *);

int main(void)
{
    char filename[20], pattern[100];
    char instr[100], *cp1, *cp2;
    int  matchct, pos, inlen;
    FILE *inp;

    printf("Enter file name ");
    gets(filename);
    printf("Enter pattern to be found ");
    gets(pattern);
```

```
        if ((inp = fopen(filename, "r")) == NULL)
        {
            printf("Cannot open input file\n");
            exit(0);
        }

        matchct = 0;
        cp2 = pattern;
        while ((fgets(instr, 100, inp)) != NULL)
        {
            // search each line until end file
            cp1 = instr;
            inlen = strlen(cp2);
            while ((pos=strpos(cp1, cp2)) >= 0)
            {
                matchct++;
                cp1 += (pos + inlen - 1);
            }
        }
        printf("%d occurrences of %s in file %s\n",
                matchct, pattern, filename);
        fclose(inp);
        return(0);
}
```

> If you're going to type this in and try it, you must include the **strpos** function from page 98.

The program **fsearch.c** uses the function **strpos**, (see page 95) to search in each line returned from the file by **fgets** for the pattern required. The arrays holding the file name and pattern are initialised after input of user data by **gets**.

fgets reads a line of the file into the array **instr**. Two local character pointers are set to the addresses of **instr** and **pattern**. If a match is found in a given line, the pointer to **instr** is incremented to allow a possible second match in that line to be found. Finally, the number of matches is reported and the file closed. This display results from a search for the pattern "*int*" in the source-code file, **fsearch.c**, itself:

```
Enter file name fsearch.c
Enter pattern to be found int
9 occurrences of int in file fsearch.c
```

Block and non-sequential I/O

Let's look at some library functions that are used for block file access. They are more general than **fgets** and **fputs**, and they allow more sophisticated operations on files. Here are the prototypes:

```
unsigned fread(void *buf, size_t n, size_t count, FILE *fp);
unsigned fwrite(void *buf, size_t n, size_t count, FILE *fp);
int fseek(FILE *fp, long n, int origin);
long ftell(FILE *fp);
int fflush(FILE *fp);
int feof(FILE *fp);
int ferror(FILE *fp);
```

The **fread** and **fwrite** functions are used for block I/O. The standard I/O functions we have used up to now do character-by-character I/O with the file buffer. **fread** reads a block of data from the standard I/O file buffer. **fwrite** writes a block of data to the buffer. For large volumes of data, this type of buffered I/O is faster than the character-based equivalent.

Where the distinction between text and binary streams is implemented, **fread** and **fwrite** may be used with either, but are usually used with binary streams.

For **fread**, **buf** is a pointer to a region of memory that will receive the data read from the file. For **fwrite**, **buf** is a pointer to the information that is to be written to the file. The number of bytes to be read or written is specified by **n**. The argument count determines how many items of **n** bytes long will be read or written. **fp** in both cases is the file pointer.

fread returns an integer value representing the number of objects read. Exception conditions following an **fread** call are checked with the functions **ferror** and **feof**.

ferror checks whether a file operation has produced an error, in which case it returns a non-zero value. Similarly, **feof** returns a non-zero value if an end-of-file condition is encountered.

fwrite returns an integer value representing the number of objects written, or a number less than count if there is an error.

fseek is used to implement a form of random access. For binary streams – and text streams, if no distinction is implemented – the function causes the file pointer to be set to a displacement of **n** characters from origin.

ftell reports the current position of the file pointer in the file, as a positive number represented as a long integer, if successful, –1 otherwise. The four functions **fread**, **fwrite**, **fseek** and **ftell** can be used in combination and built on to give the appearance of random-access or database-like functionality.

fflush causes the contents of any buffered but unwritten data to be written to the file pointed to by **fp**.

Example – creating a record-based file

The program that follows is called **recordio.c** and uses block I/O functions to create a file of 'records' from data input by the user; it then dumps to standard output the contents of the file.

Block I/O file operations

```
/*************************************************************************
 *
 *   Program 'recordio.c' — creates file called 'file.dat', using 'fwrite',
 *   from user input and dumps contents to standard output.
 *
 *   ***********************************************************************/
#include <stdio.h>
#include <stdlib.h>
#define NOT_OK 1
#define OK 0

struct file_rec
{
    char    fname[15];
    char    lname[15];
    int     age;
};
```

```c
//      Function prototype declarations

int f_create(void);
int f_display(void);
void disp_stdout(struct file_rec *);

int main(void)
{
    if ((f_create()) == NOT_OK)
    {
        printf("Couldn't create output file\n");
        exit(0);
    }

    fflush(stdin);
    printf("\nThe file will now be displayed\n");

    if ((f_display()) == NOT_OK)
    {
        printf("Couldn't display file input\n");
        exit(0);
    }
    return(0);
}

int f_create(void)
{
    struct file_rec buf;
    FILE *outp;
    int c;

    // Create output file

    if ((outp = fopen ("file.dat","wb")) == NULL)
    {
        printf("Couldn't open output file\n");
        return(NOT_OK);
    }
```

```
        do
        {
            // Enter one record of data
            printf("Enter first name, last name and age: ");
            scanf("%s %s %d", buf.fname, buf.lname, &buf.age);

            // Get rid of any unwanted scanf stuff
            fflush(stdin);

            // Write the record to the file
            if ((fwrite(&buf, sizeof(buf), 1, outp)) < 1)
            {
                printf("Can't write to output file\n");
                return(NOT_OK);
            }

            printf("Type RETURN to continue,'q' to quit: ");
        }
        while ((c = getchar()) != 'q');

        fclose(outp);
        return(OK);
    }

    int f_display(void)
    {
        struct file_rec buf;
        FILE *inp;
        int end_of_file = 0;

        if ((inp = fopen("file.dat","rb")) == NULL)
        {
            printf("Can't open file input\n");
            return(NOT_OK);
        }

        while (end_of_file == 0)
        {
            fread(&buf, sizeof(buf), 1, inp);
```

```
            if ((ferror(inp)) != 0)
            {
                printf("Error reading file\n");
                return(NOT_OK);
            }
            if ((feof(inp)) != 0)
            {
                printf("End of file reached\n");
                end_of_file = 1;
            }
            else
                disp_stdout(&buf);
        }
        fclose(inp);
        return(OK);
}

void disp_stdout(struct file_rec *pbuf)
{
    printf("\nName: %s %s\n", pbuf->fname, pbuf->lname);
    printf("Age: %d\n", pbuf->age);
}
```

The **main** function of **recordio.c** carries out two tasks: create the file **file.dat**, and dump the file to standard output.

The function **f_create** is called to create **file.dat** and to initialise it with data input by the user. The file is set up as a sequence of 'records' defined by the structure type **struct file_rec**. Recall that C has no concept of 'file record' as an inherent part of a file; here the conceptual 'record' is an arbitrary data structure, **struct file_rec**, that you define.

In **f_create**, the file is opened as a binary stream in write mode. The formatted input function **scanf** is repeatedly called and accepts user-input data, which is stored in the structure **buf** and which is then used as a record to write to the file using the **fwrite** function. The whole sequence is repeated until directed otherwise by the user.

fwrite, on error, returns an integral value less than the count of items to be written, in this case 1. **fwrite** uses the address of the structure

buf as its output buffer area. The size of the buffer to be written is found using the **sizeof** operator.

Finally, when all data has been written to the file, **file.dat** is closed with **fclose**.

The function **f_display** opens **file.dat** in read mode and repeatedly calls **fread** to read into its buffer buf records previously written. The function **p_stdout** is used on each iteration to dump the contents of **buf** to the standard output.

Here is a sample of the full interaction that happens when you use this program (user input in boldface):

```
Enter first name, last name and age: Mikhail Gorbachev  54
Type RETURN to continue,'q' to quit:
Enter first name, last name and age: Franklin Roosevelt 63
Type RETURN to continue,'q' to quit:
Enter first name, last name and age: Winston Churchill 91
Type RETURN to continue,'q' to quit:
Enter first name, last name and age: Nelson Mandela 78
Type RETURN to continue,'q' to quit:

The file will now be displayed

Name: Mikhail Gorbachev
Age: 54

Name: Franklin Roosevelt
Age: 63

Name: Winston Churchill
Age: 91

Name: Nelson Mandela
Age: 78
End of file reached
```

Any error condition resulting from **fread** is tested for, using **ferror**; **feof** otherwise reports end-of-file. When end-of-file is reached, the file is closed, control returned to **main** and the program stops.

Character class tests

The standard header file **ctype.h** provides a set of useful functions that perform tests on single-character data in a way that is not system-dependent. Suppose that, on a system which uses the ASCII character set, you made the following test:

```
char c;
    ...
/*   initialise  c  here     */
    ...
if ((c >= 'a') && (c <= 'z'))
    printf ("Lower-case alphabetic\n");
```

The test will be successful and the message printed when it should be. If the system uses the EBCDIC character set however, the test will not work because the characters from 'a' to 'z' in EBCDIC are not numerically contiguous.

The functions in **ctype.h** collectively provide a character-class programming interface that is independent of such problems. All of the functions return a non-zero integer value representing TRUE, and a zero value for FALSE. They all take one argument of type **int**, which is treated as a character.

Here's a list of the functions:

int isalpha(int c)	alphabetic: a - z, A - Z
int isalnum(int c)	alphabetic or digit
int islower(int c)	lower case: a - z
int isupper(int c)	upper case: A - Z
int isdigit (int c)	digit: 0 - 9
int isspace(int c)	blank
int iscntrl(int c)	control character, including DEL
int isgraph(int c)	like isprint, except false for space
int isxdigit(int c)	hexadecimal digit: 0 - 9, a - f, A - F
int isprint(int c)	any printable character
int ispunct(int c)	not alphanumeric or control or space

Tip

See Chapter 9 for more on these.

Exercises

1. Modify the program **filecopy.c** (page 142) so that it uses command-line arguments rather than prompts to get the names of the files involved in the copy operation.

2. Similarly, change **fsearch.c**, (page 145), to take command-line arguments.

3. Modify the program **recordio.c**(page 148) so that, instead of simply displaying the full contents of the file after the data has been entered, the user can choose the record number that the display should start from. .

Tip

You'll need to use the **fseek** function and to divide the number of bytes in the file by the record length to navigate the file in this way. Call the resulting program **randio.c**

9 C library functions

stdio.h

void clearerr(FILE *fp);
clears end-of-file and error indicators for the file pointed to by fp.

int fclose(FILE *fp);
discards any buffered input or output for the file pointed to by fp and then closes the file. It returns zero for successful file closure or EOF on error.

int feof(FILE *fp);
returns non-zero if the end of the file pointed to by fp has been reached; otherwise zero is returned.

int ferror(FILE *fp);
checks if a file operation has produced an error. It returns non-zero if an error occurred during the last operation on the file pointed to by fp, zero otherwise.

int fflush(FILE *fp);
causes the contents of any buffered but unwritten data to be written to the file pointed to by fp. The function returns zero if successful, EOF on failure.

int fgetc(FILE *fp);
returns the next character from the file pointed to by fp. It returns EOF on error or end-of-file.

int fgetpos(FILE *fp, fpos_t *ptr);
stores in the pointer ptr the current position in the file pointed to by fp. The type fpos_t is defined in stdio.h. It returns non-zero on error.

char *fgets(char *s, int n, FILE *fp);
reads a string from the file pointed to by fp until a newline character is encountered or n - 1 characters have been read. If a newline is encountered it is included in the string s which is in any event null-terminated. The function returns s, or NULL on end-of-file or error.

FILE *fopen(const char *s, const char *mode);
opens the file named in the string s in accordance with the open mode specified in the string mode. Legal modes are "r", "w" and "a" for reading, writing and appending; any of these suffixed with a + additionally opens the file for reading and writing. If a b is suffixed to the mode string a binary file is indicated. fopen returns a pointer to the file opened or NULL on error.

int fprintf(FILE *fp, const char *<format>, ...);
is the same as printf, but writes its output to the file pointed to by fp.

int fputc(int c, FILE *fp);
writes the character c to the file pointed to by fp. It returns c, or EOF on error. Although c is defined as an integer, it is treated as an unsigned char in that only the low-order byte is used.

int fputs(const char *s, FILE *fp);
writes the string s to the file pointed to by fp. The function returns a non-negative number, or EOF on error.

size_t fread(void *buf, size_t n, size_t count, FILE *fp);
reads, from the file pointed to by fp into the array at buf, up to count objects of size n. The function returns the number of objects read.

FILE *freopen(const char *s, const char *mode, FILE *fp);
opens the file named in the string s and associates with it the file pointer fp. The function returns that file pointer or NULL on error.

int fscanf(FILE *fp, const char *<format>, ...);
is the same as scanf, except that the input is read from the file pointed to by fp.

int fseek(FILE *fp, long n, int origin);
is usually used with binary streams. It causes the file position for the file pointed to by fp to be set to a displacement of n characters from origin. origin may be any of three macro values defined in stdio.h: SEEK_SET(start of file), SEEK_CUR(current position in file) or SEEK_END(end-of-file). Used with text streams, n must be zero, or a return value from ftell with origin set to SEEK_SET. The function returns non-zero on error.

int fsetpos(FILE *fp, const fpos_t *ptr);
returns the position of fp to the position stored by fgetpos in ptr. The function returns non-zero on error.

long ftell(FILE *fp);
returns the current file position for the file pointed to by fp, or -1L on error.

size_t fwrite(void *buf, size_t n, size_t count, FILE *fp);
causes count objects of size n bytes to be written from buf to the file pointed to by fp and returns the number of such objects written. A number less than count is returned on error.

int getc(FILE *fp);
reads the next character from the file pointed to by fp and returns it, or EOF on end-of-file or error. getc is a macro and equivalent to fgetc.

int getchar(void);
reads the next character from standard input and returns that character, or EOF on end-of-file or error. getchar() is functionally equivalent to getc(stdin).

char *gets(char *s);
reads from standard input an input line into the array at s, replacing the terminating newline with a null terminator. The string s is also returned by gets, or a null pointer on end-of-file or error.

void perror(const char *s);
displays on the standard error device the string s, followed by a colon and an error message generated from the contents of the value of the external variable errno which has a corresponding declaration in errno.h.

int printf(const char *<format>, ...);
writes to standard output the contents of the format string, other than special control sequences contained in the format string, followed by the contents of a list of variables converted according to the control sequences in the format string. These are the printf format codes and their meanings:

d, i, o, u x, X The variable corresponding to the format code is converted to decimal (d,i), octal (o), unsigned decimal (u) or unsigned hexadecimal (x and X). The x conversion uses the letters abcdef; X uses ABCDEF.

f The variable is converted to a decimal notation of form [-]ddd.ddd, where the minimum width (w) of the field and the precision (p) are specified by %w.pf. The default precision is 6 characters; a precision of zero causes the decimal point to be suppressed.

e, E The float or double variable is converted to scientific notation of form [-]d.ddde±dd. Width and precision may also be specified. The default precision is 6 characters; a precision of zero causes the decimal point to be suppressed.

g, G The float or double variable is printed in style f or e. Style e is used only if the exponent resulting from the conversion is less than −4 or greater than or equal to the precision. Trailing zeros are removed. A decimal point appears only if it is followed by a digit.

c	The variable is displayed as a character.
s	The variable is taken to be a string (character pointer) and characters from the string are displayed until a null character is encountered or the number of characters indicated by the precision specification is reached.
p	Display variable as a pointer of type void *.
n	The associated variable is a pointer to an integer which is assigned the number of characters displayed so far by printf on this call.
%	Display a literal %.

A range of *modifiers* may be used with the format codes to specify the field width, signing and justification, precision and length of the output.

An integer between the percent sign and the format code specifies the minimum width of the output field. The output is padded, if necessary, with spaces, or with zeros if the integer is prefixed with a 0.

All output is, by default, right-justified; it can be left-justified by insertion of a - before the format code (and minimum width specifier, if any). Similar insertion of a + ensures the number is printed with a sign; a space character causes a space to prefix the output if there is no sign.

Precision is specified if the minimum width specifier is followed by a full-stop and an integer. The integer specifies the display of the maximum number of characters from a string, or the minimum number of digits for an integer, or the number of decimal places, or the number of significant digits for output of floating-point data.

Length modifiers h, l and L are available. h causes the corresponding variable to be printed as a short; l as a long and L as a long double.

int putc(int c, FILE *fp);
writes the character c to the file pointed to by fp and returns it; it returns EOF on error. putc is a macro and is equivalent to fputc.

int putchar(int c);
writes the next character to standard output and returns that character, or EOF on error. putchar(c) is functionally equivalent to putc(c, stdout).

int puts(const char *s);
writes the string s to the standard output, followed by a newline. The function returns EOF on error, otherwise a zero or positive number.

int remove(const char *s);
erases the file named in the string s, returning zero on success, non-zero on error.

int rename(const char *s1, const char *s2);
changes the name of the file named in string s1 to the name in s2, returning zero on success, non-zero on error.

void rewind(FILE *fp);
resets the file position indicator to the start of the file pointed to by fp.

int scanf(const char *<format>, ...);
reads from the standard input data which is converted and stored in memory at the addresses specified by a number of pointer variables in the variable list. Conversions are performed according to the format string specifications corresponding to the individual variables. Ordinary (non-format specifier) characters in the format string must correspond to the next non-whitespace character of input. These are the scanf format codes:

d, i, o,u, x	Read a decimal, integer, octal, unsigned or hexadecimal number from standard input and place at an integer pointer given in the argument list.
e, f, g	Read a floating-point number and place at a float pointer specified in the argument list.
c, s	Read: (c) a number of characters (default 1); (s) a string. In both cases place the input at a character pointer specified in the argument list.
p	Read a pointer(of type void *, as output by printf) and place at a pointer specified in the argument list.
n	Assign to the associated argument (int *) the number of characters so far read by this call.
[ ]	Read the longest string of input characters from the scan set between brackets and place at a character pointer specified in the argument list. A null terminator is added.
[^]	Read the longest set of input characters not from the scan set between brackets and place at a character

pointer specified in the argument list. A null terminator is added.

%   Literal %; no assignment.

A range of *modifiers* may be used with the format codes to suppress assignment of input and to specify maximum field length.

An asterisk between the percent sign and the format code causes the input field corresponding to the format code to be discarded.

Maximum field width is specified by an integer after the % sign in the format string. Input characters effectively truncated by the maximum value will be stored at the next variable, if any, in the variable list.

Length modifiers h, l and L are available. h causes the input to be stored at a pointer to a variable of type short. l causes input to be stored at a pointer to a variable of type long, or to modify the effect of the %f, %g and %e specifiers so that the input is assigned to a pointer to a variable of type double. L causes input to be stored at a long double.

void setbuf(FILE *fp, char *s);
sets the buffer for the file pointed to by fp to s; full buffering is specified. If s is NULL, buffering is turned off for the file.

int setvbuf(FILE *fp, char *s, int m, size_t size);
allows different types of buffering to be specified for the file pointed to by fp. Symbolic-constant buffering modes, which are supplied as arguments to m, are defined in stdio.h. _IOFBF, _IOLBF and _IONBF cause full, line and no buffering respectively. If s is not null, it is used as the file buffer, with buffer size determined by size. The function returns non-zero on error.

int sprintf(char *s, const char *<format>, ...);
is the same as printf except that its output is written to the string pointed to by s, which is null-terminated.

int sscanf(char *s, const char *<format>, ...);
is the same as scanf except that the input is read from the string pointed to by s.

FILE *tmpfile(void);
returns a pointer to a temporary file of access mode "wb+" which is automatically removed on closure. The function returns NULL on error.

char *tmpnam(char *s);
If s is NULL, tmpnam generates a string which is not the name of an existing file and returns a pointer to an internal static array. If s is not NULL, the name string is additionally stored in s.

int ungetc(int c, FILE *fp);
returns the character c to the file pointed to by fp; c will be returned on the next read. It returns the character returned or EOF on error.

int vfprintf(FILE *fp, const char *<format>, va_list arg);
is the same as fprintf except that arg is initialised with the argument list by the va_start macro defined in stdarg.h.

int vprintf(const char *<format>, va_list arg);
is the same as printf except that arg is initialised with the argument list by the va_start macro defined in stdarg.h.

int vsprintf(char *s, const char *<format>, va_list arg);
is the same as sprintf except that arg is initialised with the argument list by the va_start macro defined in stdarg.h.

Tip

If you want to find out more about C's functions — and much else besides — see the Newnes C Pocket Book, second edition.

string.h

void *memchr(const void *s, unsigned char c, size_t n);
returns a pointer to the first occurrence of the character c within the first n characters of the array s. The function returns NULL if there is no match. The type size_t is defined in stddef.h as an unsigned integer.

int memcmp(const void *s1, const void *s2, size_t n);
compares the first n characters of s1 with those of s2 and returns an integer less than, equal to or greater than zero depending on whether s1 is lexicographically less than, equal to or greater than s2.

void *memcpy(void *outs, const void *ins, size_t n);
causes n characters to be copied from the array ins to the array outs. The function returns a pointer to outs.

void *memmove(void *outs, const void *ins, size_t n);
causes n characters to be copied from the array ins to the array outs, additionally allowing the copy to take place even if the objects being copied overlap in memory. The function returns a pointer to outs.

void *memset(void *s, unsigned char c, size_t n);
causes the first n characters of the array s to be filled with the character c. The function returns a pointer to s.

char *strcat(char *s1, const char *s2);
appends a copy of string s2 to the end of s1 and returns a pointer to the null-terminated result.

char *strchr(const char *s, int c);
returns a pointer to the first occurrence of character c in string s or a null pointer if c does not occur in s.

int strcmp(const char *s1, const char *s2);
compares the arguments and returns an integer less than, equal to or greater than zero depending on whether s1 is lexicographically less than, equal to or greater than s2.

char *strcpy(char *s1, const char *s2);
copies string s2 to s1, stopping after the null character has been copied and returning a pointer to s1.

size_t strcspn(const char *s1, const char *s2);
returns the length of the initial segment of the string s1 which consists entirely of characters not in s2.

char *strerror(size_t n);
returns a pointer to a string corresponding to a system-dependent error number n.

size_t strlen(const char *s);
returns the number of characters in s, not counting the null-terminator.

char *strncat(char *s1, const char *s2, int n);
appends at most n characters from s2 to s1 and returns a pointer to the null-terminated result.

int strncmp(const char *s1, const char *s2, int n);
is the same as strcmp, but compares at most n characters.

char *strncpy(char *s1, const char *s2, int n);
copies exactly n characters, truncating s2 or adding null characters to s1 if necessary. The result is not null-terminated if the length of s2 is n or more. A pointer to s1 is returned.

char *strpbrk(const char *s1, const char *s2);
returns a pointer to the first occurrence in string s1 of any character from string s2, or a NULL character if there is no match.

char *strrchr(const char *s, int c);
is the same as strchr except that a pointer to the last occurrence of the character in the string is returned.

size_t strspn(const char *s1, const char *s2);
returns the length of the initial segment of s1 which consists entirely of characters from s2.

char *strstr(const char *s1, const char *s2);
returns a pointer to the first occurrence of s2 in s1, or NULL if there is no match.

ctype.h

int **isalnum(int c)**;
returns non-zero if c is alphanumeric, zero otherwise.

int **isalpha(int c)**;
returns non-zero if c is alphabetic, zero otherwise.

int **iscntrl(int c)**;
returns non-zero if c is a control character (0 to 037, or DEL (0177), in the ASCII set), zero otherwise.

int **isdigit(int c)**;
returns non-zero if c is a digit, zero otherwise.

int **isgraph(int c)**;
returns non-zero if c is a printable character other than a space, zero otherwise.

int **islower(int c)**;
returns non-zero if c is a lowercase letter in the range a to z, zero otherwise.

int **isprint(int c)**;
returns non-zero if c is a printable character including space, zero otherwise.

int **ispunct(int c)**;
returns non-zero if c is a printable character other than space, letter and digit, zero otherwise.

int **isspace(int c)**;
returns non-zero if c is any of space, tab, vertical tab, carriage return, newline or formfeed, zero otherwise.

int **isupper(int c)**;
returns non-zero if c is an upper-case letter in the range A to Z, zero otherwise.

int **isxdigit(int c)**;
returns non-zero if c is a hexadecimal digit in the range a to f, A to F, or 0 to 9, zero otherwise.

int **tolower(int c)**;
converts c to lower-case and returns c.

int **toupper(int c)**;
converts c to upper-case and returns c.

math.h

For the functions declared in math.h, there is a macro, also defined in math.h, called HUGE_VAL. If any of the math.h functions produces a value too large to be stored in a variable of type double, HUGE_VAL is returned, signifying a *range error*. If the input to any of the math.h functions is not in the required domain, a *domain error* is the result; the function return value is implementation-dependent.

double acos(double x);
returns the arccosine of x in the range zero to PI.

double asin(double x);
returns the arcsine of x in the range –PI/2 to PI/2.

double atan(double x);
returns the arctangent of x in the range –PI/2 to PI/2.

double atan2(double y, double x);
returns the arctangent of y/x in the range –PI to PI, using the signs of both arguments to determine the quadrant of the return value.

double ceil(double x);
returns, as a double, the smallest integer which is not less than x.

double cos(double x);
returns the cosine of x in radians.

double cosh(double x);
returns the hyperbolic cosine of x.

double exp(double x);
returns the value of e raised to the power of x.

double fabs(double x);
returns the absolute value of x.

double floor(double x);
returns, as a double, the largest integer which is not greater than x.

double fmod(double x, double y);
returns the remainder of the division of x by y. If y is zero, the result is undefined.

double frexp(double x, int *exp);
splits a floating-point number x in two parts: a fraction f and an exponent n such that f is either zero or in the range 0.5 and 1.0 and x equals f*(2**n). The fraction is returned and the exponent n stored at exp. If x is initially zero, the returned parameters are also both zero.

double log(double x);
returns as a double floating-point number the natural logarithm of x.

double log10(double x);
returns as a double floating-point number the logarithm to base 10 of x.

double modf(double x, double *iptr);
returns the integral part of x at the double pointer iptr. The function returns the fractional part of x.

double pow(double x, double y);
returns as a double floating-point number the value of x raised to the power of y.

double ldexp(double x, int n);
returns as a double floating-point number the result of x *(2**n).

double sin(double x);
returns the sine of x in radians.

double sinh(double x);
returns the hyperbolic sine of x.

double sqrt(double x);
returns the non-negative square root of x; the value of x must not be negative.

double tan(double x);
returns the tangent of x in radians.

double tanh(double x);
returns the hyperbolic tangent of x.

stdlib.h

void abort(void);
causes abnormal program termination.

int abs(int num);
returns the absolute value of the integer num.

int atexit(void(*f)(void));
causes the function f to be called if the program terminates normally and returns non-zero if the function cannot be called.

double atof(const char *s);
converts and returns as a double floating point number the string at s, returning zero on error.

int atoi(const char *s);
converts and returns as an integer the string at s, returning zero on error.

int atol(const char *s);
converts and returns as a long integer the string at s, or zero on error.

void *bsearch(const void *key, const void *base, size_t n, size_t size, int(*comp)(const void *key, const void *element));
does a binary search on the sorted array pointed to by base and returns a pointer to the first member which matches key. The number of array elements is specified by n and the size in bytes of each element by size. The type size_t is defined as unsigned int in stddef.h. comp compares elements in turn with key. If key is not matched, NULL is returned.

void *calloc(size_t n, size_t size);
allocates space in memory for n objects, each of size size. The function returns a pointer to the allocated memory (which, unlike with malloc, is zero-initialised), or NULL if the memory could not be allocated.

div_t div(int n, int d);
calculates the quotient and remainder of n/d. The results are stored in the int members quot and rem of a structure of type div_t. The type div_t is defined in stdlib.h.

void exit(int status);
causes immediate normal program termination. The value of status is returned to the operating system environment. Zero status is treated as indicating normal termination.

void free(void *p);
deallocates the memory pointed to by p and makes it available for other use. Before free is called, memory must have been allocated and p initialised by one of the library functions malloc, calloc or realloc. According to the ISO specifications, free should work but do nothing when p is NULL.

char *getenv(const char *s);
returns the operating-system environment string associated with the identifier named in the string at s. If no value is associated with the name in s, getenv returns a null pointer. Further details are system-dependent.

long labs(long n);
returns as a long integer the absolute value of the long integer n.

ldiv_t ldiv(int n, int d);
calculates the quotient and remainder of n/d. The results are stored in the long members quot and rem of a structure of type ldiv_t. The type ldiv_t is defined in stdlib.h.

void *malloc(size_t size);
allocates space in memory for an object with size (in bytes) of size. The function returns a pointer to the allocated memory, or NULL if the memory could not be allocated. Memory allocated by malloc is not initialised to any particular value.

void qsort(void *base, size_t n, size_t size, int(*comp)(const void *key, const void *element));
sorts the array pointed to by base, which contains n elements of size size, using the recursive Quicksort algorithm. The function comp compares elements in turn with key and returns a negative, zero or positive integer depending on whether key is less than, equal to or greater than element.

int rand(void);
returns a (pseudo) random number in the range zero to at least 32,767.

void *realloc(void *ptr, size_t size);
changes the size in memory for the object pointed to by ptr to size. The function returns a pointer to the reallocated memory, or NULL if the memory could not be reallocated. If NULL is returned, the value of ptr is unchanged. realloc(ptr, 0); deallocates all memory at ptr, replacing it with nothing. This form is equivalent to free(ptr);.

void srand(unsigned int seed);
generates a new set of (pseudo) random numbers using seed, which
has an initial value of 1, as the seed.

double strtod(const char *s, char **ptr);
returns as a double floating-point number the value represented by
the character string pointed to by s. An optional string of white space
characters, an optional sign, a string of digits optionally containing a
decimal point, and an optional e or E followed by an optional sign are
recognised by strtod. strtod scans the input string up to the first
unrecognised character; if the contents of ptr are not NULL, a pointer
to the character terminating the scan is stored in *ptr. atof(s) is
equivalent to strtod(s,(char **)0).

char *strtok(char *s1, const char *s2);
considers the string s1 to consist of a sequence of zero or more text
tokens separated by spans of one or more characters from the
separator string s2. The function is called iteratively, returning pointers
to tokens extracted from s1 and delimited by a character from s2.
strtok returns NULL when it finds no further tokens.

long strtol(const char *s, char **ptr, int base);
returns as a long integer the value represented by the character string
pointed to by s. Leading white space is ignored. The string is scanned
up to the first character inconsistent with the base. If the contents of
ptr are not NULL, a pointer to the character terminating the scan is
stored in *ptr. If no integer can be formed, that location is set to s and
zero is returned. If base is zero, the base to be used is calculated
automatically. Otherwise, the base must not be negative or greater
than 36. Any overflow or underflow conditions cause a return value of
LONG_MAX or LONG_MIN, defined in limits.h.

unsigned long strtoul(const char *s, char **ptr, int base);
is the same as strtol except for its return type and its error return
values of ULONG_MAX and ULONG_MIN.

10 Answers to exercises

Chapter 1

1. Prototype (declaration), call and definition (function header and body). Program **func.c** follows.

    ```c
    #include <stdio.h>

    void proto(void);          // prototype

    void main(void)
    {
      proto();     // call
    }

    void proto(void)           // definition
    {
      printf("In function proto\n");
    }
    ```

2. Program **structio.c**:

    ```c
    #include <stdio.h>
    #include <stdlib.h>

    struct partrec
    {
      char partno[8];
      char partname[30];
      double partprice;
    };

    int main(void)
    {
      char temp[10];
      struct partrec item;

      printf("Enter part number: ");
      gets(item.partno);
      printf("Enter part name: ");
      gets(item.partname);
      printf("Enter part price: ");
      gets(temp);
      item.partprice = atof(temp);

      printf("Item data entered:\n");
      printf("Part number %s\n", item.partno);
      printf("Part name %s\n", item.partname);
      printf("Part price %f\n", item.partprice);

      return(0);
    }
    ```

3. The test if (s = 2) always goes true (because 2, being non-zero, is true) and the two **printf**s are executed regardless of the initial value of **s**. To make the test a *test* as opposed to an *assignment*, use the equality-test operator ==.

4. Program **oddloop.c**:

    ```c
    #include <stdio.h>

    void main(void)
    {
      int i;
      for (i = 1; i < 100; i = i + 2)
        printf("Value of i: %d\n", i);
    }
    ```

5. Program **intptr.c**:

    ```c
    #include <stdio.h>

    void main(void)
    {
      int i = 5;
      int *ip;

      ip = &i;
      printf("Object at the pointer is: %d\n", *ip);
    }
    ```

Chapter 2

1. Here's the modified program, **sum1ton.c**:

    ```c
    #include <stdio.h>
    #include <stdlib.h>

    int main(void)
    {
      char asciiN[20];
      long n, sum1toN;
      printf("Enter a number: ");
      gets(asciiN);
      n = atol(asciiN);
      sum1toN = (n * (n + 1))/2;
      printf("Sum of the integer series 1 to %ld is: %ld\n", n, sum1toN);
      return(0);
    }
    ```

2. They don't come much shorter than **escpath.c**:

    ```
    #include <stdio.h>

    void main(void)
    {
      printf("Pathname is C:\\MSVC\\BIN\n");
    }
    ```

3. The same principle holds for escstr.c:

    ```
    #include <stdio.h>

    void main(void)
    {
      printf("String is \"String1\",\"String2\"\n");
    }
    ```

4. The program is called **sqroot.c**, the answer is about 81 (1.732050808 being approximately the square root of 3) and the format code specification **14.10** displays a width of 14 and up to 10 decimal places.

    ```
    #include <stdio.h>

    void main(void)
    {
      int i;
      double r = 1.732050808;

      printf("Before multiply %14.10f\n", r);

      for (i = 1; i <= 3; i = i + 1)
        r = r * r;
      printf("After multiply %14.10f\n", r);
    }
    ```

5. The program is addchar.c and the result of the addition is the letter 'o' (after you've adjusted for a base value of 'a').

    ```
    #include <stdio.h>

    int main(void)
    {
      char c1 = 'g', c2 = 'h';

      printf("Chars are %c and %c, sum is %c\n", c1, c2, c1+c2-'a'+1);

      return(0);
    }
    ```

174

Chapter 3

1. Here's the accumulator program, **accum.c**:

```c
#include <stdio.h>

void run_total(int);
int main(void)
{
  int count;

  for (count = 1; count <= 5; count = count + 1)
  {
    run_total(count);
  }
  return(0);
}

void run_total(int increment)
{
  static int accum = 0;
  accum = accum + increment;
  printf("Value of accumulator is now %d\n", accum);
}
```

2. The program **ptrarg.c** calls a function with an indirected argument and displays the changed value of the argument after the call.

```c
#include <stdio.h>
#include <stdlib.h>          // declares atoi

void get_num(int *);

int main(void)
{
  int arg;

  get_num(&arg);
  printf("New value is: %d\n", arg);
  return(0);
}

void get_num(int *argp)
{
  char instr[30];

  printf("Enter a number: ");

  *argp = atoi(gets(instr));  // Note the nested function call!
}
```

3. The program **ioscanf.c** does the job:

```
#include <stdio.h>

void get_num(int *);

int main(void)
{
  int arg;
  get_num(&arg);
  printf("New value is: %d\n", arg);
  return(0);
}

void get_num(int *argp)
{
  char instr[30];
  printf("Enter a number: ");
  scanf("%d", argp);
}
```

Chapter 4

1. The program **macro.c** implements the required macro:

```
#include <stdio.h>

// macro
#define MIN(a, b) (a < b) ? a : b

int main(void)
{
  int first, second;
  printf("Enter two integer numbers ");
  scanf("%d %d", &first, &second);
  printf("Smaller of the two numbers is %d\n", MIN(first, second));
  return(0);
}
```

2. The function validate fails because the April/June/September/November test is wrongly parenthesised:

```
int validate(int yy, int mm, int dd)
{
  //    Validate the date entered according to the well-known rules
  if ((yy < MINYY) || (yy > MAXYY))
    return (FALSE);
```

```
    if ((mm < MINMM) || (mm > MAXMM))
      return (FALSE);
    if ((dd < MINDD) || (dd > MAXDD))
      return (FALSE);

    // && evaluated first. If mm is 4 or 6 or 9, return FALSE
    // regardless of the value of dd. 27/06/95 (wrongly) fails
    if (mm==4 || mm==6 || mm==9 || mm==11 && (dd > (MAXDD - 1)))

    // correct form follows
    // if ((mm==4 || mm==6 || mm==9 || mm==11) && (dd > (MAXDD - 1)))
    //    return (FALSE);
    // If the month is February and the year divisible evenly by 4, we have
    // a leap year, unless the year is 00. 1900 was not a leap year; 2000 is.
    if (mm == 2)
    {
      if (dd > MAXFEB)
          return(FALSE);
      if (((yy % 4) != 0) || (yy == MINYY))
        if (dd > MINFEB)
          return(FALSE);
    }
    //     valid date
    return(TRUE);
  }
```

3. The statement as shown gets a character (using **getchar**) from the standard input, compares that character for equality with the character 'q' and then assigns the truth (1) or falsehood (0) of the equality test to **c**. What is required to assign the character read to **c** is this:

```
while (( c = getchar()) ! = 'q')
```

4. The modified **dates.h**/**validate.c** combination following does the more rigorous date validation. It tests for the full definition of a leap year as well as the September 1752 gap. First, we have **dates.h**:

```
#define JULGREG 1752
#define MINYY   0
#define MAXYY   9999
#define MINYY   0
#define MINMM   1
#define MAXMM   12
#define MINDD   1
#define MAXDD   31
#define MINFEB  28
#define MAXFEB  29
#define TRUE    1
#define FALSE   0
```

// Function prototype declarations follow

```c
void  get_data(int *, int *, int *);
int  validate(int, int, int);
```

and this is followed by the program logic, contained in the file **validate.c**:

```c
#include <stdio.h>
#include <stdlib.h>
#include "dates.h"

// Function prototype declarations follow
void  get_data(int *, int *, int *);
int   validate(int, int, int);

int main(void)
{
  int c, yy, mm, dd;

  get_data(&yy, &mm, &dd);

  // Check date for correctness. 0-9999 year assumed.
  if (validate(yy, mm, dd))
    printf ("Date entered is valid\n\n");
  else
    printf ("Invalid date entered\n\n");
  return(0);
}

void get_data(int *pyy, int *pmm, int *pdd)
{
  printf("Enter a date of form dd/mm/yyyy: ");
  scanf("%d/%d/%d",pdd, pmm, pyy);
}

int validate(int yy, int mm, int dd)
{
  //     Validate the date entered according to the well-known rules
  if (yy == JULGREG)
    if ((mm == 9) && (dd > 2) && (dd < 14))
      return(FALSE);
  if ((yy < MINYY) || (yy > MAXYY))
    return (FALSE);
  if ((mm < MINMM) || (mm > MAXMM))
    return (FALSE);
  if ((dd < MINDD) || (dd > MAXDD))
    return (FALSE);
```

```
if ((mm==4) || (mm==6) || (mm==9) || (mm==11))
  if (dd > (MAXDD - 1))
    return (FALSE);

//    If the month is February and the year is divisible evenly by 4
//    or 400 but not just by 100, it's a leap year.
if (mm == 2)
{
  if (dd > MAXFEB)
    return(FALSE);
  if ((yy % 4) != 0) // not a leap year
    if (dd > MINFEB)
      return(FALSE);
  // divisible by 100 but not 400, not a leap year
  if (((yy % 100) == 0) && ((yy % 400) != 0))
    if (dd > MINFEB)
      return(FALSE);
}
//    valid date
return(TRUE);
}
```

Chapter 5

1. Here are minimal examples of the three infinite-loop forms, using, respectively, the **for**, **while** and **do...while** constructs:

    ```
    // infinite 'for' loop
    for(;;);

    // infinite 'while' loop
    int x = 0;
    while(x == 0)
      ;
    // infinite 'do...while' loop
    do
    {
    }while(x == 0);
    ```

2. The program **switch.c** acknowledges input of all numbers in the range $1 - 5$ and rejects all others:

    ```
    #include <stdio.h>

    int main(void)
    {
      int c;
    ```

```
        printf("Enter a single-digit number: ");
        c = getchar();

        switch (c)
        {
          case '1':  printf("One\n");
                     break;
          case '2':  printf("Two\n");
                     break;
          case '3':  printf("Three\n");
                     break;
          case '4':  printf("Four\n");
                     break;
          case '5':  printf("Five\n");
                     break;
          default :  printf("Invalid number input\n");
                     break;
        }
      return 0;
    }
```

3.   Here's the full **dates.c** program. See also *The C Pocket Book*, second edition. Note the the program consists of two files, the header file **dates.h** and the program file **dates.c**. The latter **#includes** the former.

```
/*
 *      Header file 'dates.h',   used in program 'dates.c'
 */
#define MINYY    0
#define MAXYY    9999
#define MINYYHI 1900
#define MAXYYLO 99
#define MINMM    1
#define MAXMM    12
#define MINDD    1
#define MAXDD    31
#define MINFEB  28
#define MAXFEB  29
#define TRUE     1
#define FALSE    0

// Function prototype declarations follow

void  get_data(int *, int *, int *);
int   validate(int, int, int *);
int   find_day(int, int, int);
void  disp_day(int, int, int, int);
```

```c
/*
 *      Sample program 'dates.c': accepts as input dates of form dd/mm/yy
 *       and dd/mm/ccyy, validates them, and returns the result of the validation
 *       as well as the date's day-of-the-week. Years 1900-9999 are valid.
 *
 */
#include <stdio.h>
#include <stdlib.h>
#include "dates.h"

int main(void)
{
   //    define three integers to hold date parts
   int dd, mm, yy;
   int c, dayofweek;
   printf("Press RETURN to start,");
   printf(" 'q'-RETURN to quit\n");
   while ((c = getchar()) != 'q')
   {

      // 'get_data' returns day, month and year values input by the user.
      get_data(&dd, &mm, &yy);
      // The 'validate' function checks for wrong dates
      if ((validate(dd, mm, &yy)) == FALSE)
      {
         printf("Invalid Date Entered\n");
         printf("Press RETURN to continue\n");
         continue;
      }

      // The 'find_day' function uses its arguments to compute the number
      // of days elapsed between 1/1/1900 and the date entered.
      // The remainder after division by 7 gives the displacement in the days
      //  of the week from Dec 31, 1899, which was a Sunday.
      dayofweek = find_day(dd, mm, yy);

      // 'disp_day' uses the integer dayofweek to display the results.
      disp_day(dayofweek, dd, mm, yy);
      printf("Press RETURN to start, ");
      printf("'q'-RETURN to quit\n");
   }
   return(0);
}

void get_data(int *dd, int *mm, int *yy)
{
   //     define arrays for date input
   char sdd[5], smm[5], syy[5];
```

```c
        printf("Enter the day number: ");
        gets(sdd);
        printf("Enter the month number: ");
        gets(smm);
        printf("Enter the year number: ");
        gets(syy);

        //   Convert the strings to numeric
        *dd = atoi(sdd);
        *mm = atoi(smm);
        *yy = atoi(syy);
}

int validate(int dd, int mm, int *yy)
{
    // Validate the date entered according to the well-known rules
    if ((*yy < MINYY) || (*yy > MAXYY))
        return(FALSE);
    // Year invalid if between 100 and 1899
    if ((*yy > MAXYYLO) && (*yy < MINYYHI))
        return(FALSE);
    if ((mm < MINMM) || (mm > MAXMM))
        return(FALSE);
    if ((dd < MINDD) || (dd > MAXDD))
        return(FALSE);
    if ((mm==4) || (mm==6) || (mm==9) || (mm==11))
        if (dd > (MAXDD - 1))
            return(FALSE);

    //   If the month is February and the year is not divisible evenly by 4,
    //   the day must not exceed 28. If the year is divisible evenly by 4
    //   and 100 but not 400  (e.g. the year 2100), it's not a leap year
    //   and the day must not exceed 28.
        if (mm == 2)
        {
            if (dd > MAXFEB)
                return(FALSE);
            if ((*yy % 4) != 0)
                if (dd > MINFEB)
                    return(FALSE);
            if (((*yy % 100) == 0) && ((*yy % 400) != 0))
                if (dd > MINFEB)
                    return(FALSE);
        }

    //   After validation, express all dates as displacements from a 1900 zero
    if (*yy >= MINYYHI)
        *yy -= MINYYHI;
    return(TRUE);            //   Return valid date indicator
}
```

```c
int find_day(int dd, int mm, int yy)
{
  short no_leaps   = 0;
  short yy_count   = 0;
  short sub        = 1;
  long int days_total = 0;
  int days_year  = 0;
  int mdd[13] = {0,31,28,31,30,31,30,31,31,30,31,30,31};

  //   Count the number of leap years since 1900
  while (yy_count < yy)
  {
    yy_count += 4;

    //   Don't increment leap count if it's 1900, 2100, 2200, 2300, 2500, ...
    if ((((yy_count+MINYYHI) % 100) == 0) &&
        (((yy_count+MINYYHI) % 400) != 0))
      continue;
    no_leaps++;
  }

  //   If date entered is a leap year later than February and if it is not 1900,
  //   2100, 2200, 2300, 2500, 2600... add 1 to the total of leap years.
  if (yy_count == yy)
    if (!(((yy_count+MINYYHI) % 100) == 0) &&
    (((yy_count+MINYYHI) % 400) != 0)))
      if (mm > 2)
        no_leaps++;
  //   Calculate the number of days in the elapsed part of the year specified.
  while (sub < mm)
  {
    days_year += mdd[sub];
    sub++;
  }

  //   Compute the total number of days since 1/1/1900
  days_total = (long)yy * 365 + no_leaps + days_year + dd;

  //   1900 was not a leap year, so subtract 1 from the leap-year total,
  //     unless the year entered was 00
  if (yy != MINYY)
    days_total--;

  return((int)(days_total % 7));
}

void disp_day(int dayofweek, int dd, int mm, int yy)
{
```

```
    yy += MINYYHI;
    switch(dayofweek)
    {
        case 1: printf("%d/%d/%d  valid,  Mon.\n",dd,mm,yy);
                break;
        case 2: printf("%d/%d/%d  valid,  Tue.\n",dd,mm,yy);
                break;
        case 3: printf("%d/%d/%d  valid,  Wed.\n",dd,mm,yy);
                break;
        case 4: printf("%d/%d/%d  valid,  Thu.\n",dd,mm,yy);
                break;
        case 5: printf("%d/%d/%d  valid,  Fri.\n",dd,mm,yy);
                break;
        case 6: printf("%d/%d/%d  valid,  Sat.\n",dd,mm,yy);
                break;
        case 0: printf("%d/%d/%d  valid,  Sun.\n",dd,mm,yy);
                break;
        default: printf("Cannot compute day of date\n");
                break;
    }
}
```

Chapter 6

1. Here is the program **scopy.c**:

```
#include <stdio.h>

int main(void)
{
    char arr1[50], arr2[50];
    char *cp1 = arr1, *cp2 = arr2;

    printf("Enter the string to be copied: ");
    gets(cp2);

    // Naive copy follows

    while(*cp2 != '\0')
    {
        *cp1 = *cp2;
        cp1++;
        cp2++;
    }
    *cp1 = '\0';
    printf("String after copy %s\n", arr1);
    return(0);
}
```

2. And here's the cool version, mincopy.c, of the same thing:

```c
#include <stdio.h>

int main(void)
{
  char arr1[50], arr2[50];
  char *cp1 = arr1, *cp2 = arr2;

  printf("Enter the string to be copied: ");
  gets(cp2);

  // Current-champion copy follows
  while(*cp1++ = *cp2++);

  printf("String after copy %s\n", arr1);
  return(0);
}
```

3. The program svalid.c validates a maximum six-digit number:

```c
#include <stdio.h>
#include <string.h>

void main(void)
{
  char arr[50];
  char *cp = arr;
  int len;
  printf("Enter a string: ");
  gets(arr);
  len = strlen(arr);
  if ((len < 1) || (len > 6))
  {
    printf("Input string of invalid length\n");
    return;
  }

  while (*cp)
  {
    if ((*cp < '0') || (*cp > '9'))
    {
      printf("Non-numeric character in string\n");
      return;
    }
    cp++;
  }
  printf("%s is a valid number\n", arr);
}
```

4. Here's how to display a string in reverse, with the program **reverse.c**:

```
#include <stdio.h>
#include <string.h>

void main(void)
{
  char arr[50];
  char *cp = arr;
  int len;

  printf("Enter a string: ");
  gets(arr);

  len = strlen(arr);

  cp += len - 1;  // set pointer to end

  printf("String in reverse: ");
  while (cp >= arr)
    printf("%c", *cp--);
}
```

Chapter 7

1. You can best see the difference between *typedef* and *preprocessor* substitution from compile-time errors:

```
#include <stdio.h>

#define PCHAR char *
typedef char * charptr;

void main(void)
{
  char c = 'x';

  // substitutes to: char *char1, char2;
  PCHAR char1, char2;
  // correctly defined as char *char1, *char2;
  charptr char3, char4;

  char1 = &c;    // OK
  char2 = &c;    // Error, char2 isn't a pointer
  char3 = &c;    // OK
  char4 = &c;    // OK
}
```

2. The program **maxint.c** is an enhanced version of the one in Chapter 2. It will find the maximum integer capacity for a 32- or 64-bit system:

```c
#include <stdio.h>

int main(void)
{
   int shift = 1, accum = 0;

   //    loop until a further shift would set the sign bit
   while(shift > 0)
   {
      //    add shift to the accumulator and double it
      accum = accum + shift;
      shift = shift * 2;
   }
   printf("Maximum int value is %d\n", accum);
   return(0);
}
```

3. This is the minimal linked-list program, **lnstruct.c**:

```c
#include <stdio.h>

struct node
{
   int    x;
   double  y;
   struct node *next;
};

int main(void)
{
   struct node first, second;
   struct node *head = &first;
   // Assign to structure members
   first.x      = 5;
   first.y      = 34.78;
   second.x   = 6;
   second.y   = 45.89;

   // Link first and second structures
   first.next   = &second;

   // Display the values of structure members
   printf("first.x: %d\n",first.x);
   printf("first.y: %f\n", first.y);
   printf("second.x: %d\n",second.x);
```

```c
        printf("second.y: %f\n", second.y);
        printf("first.next->x:  %d\n",first.next->x);
        printf("first.next->y:  %f\n", first.next->y);

        // Display the values of linked structure members
        printf("head->x: %d\n",head->x);
        printf("head->y: %f\n", head->y);
        printf("head->next->x:  %d\n",head->next->x);
        printf("head->next->y:  %f\n", head->next->y);

        return(0);
    }
```

4. **dynstruc.c** does the same as **lnstruct.c**, but uses dynamic allocation to get memory for the list nodes.

```c
#include <stdio.h>
#include <stdlib.h>

struct node
{
  int    x;
  double  y;
  struct node *next;
};

int main(void)
{
  struct node *head;

  if ((head = (struct node *)malloc(sizeof(struct node))) == NULL)
  {
    printf("Memory error allocating list head\n");
    exit(0);
  }

  if ((head->next = (struct node *)malloc(sizeof(struct node))) == NULL)
  {
    printf("Memory error allocating list next element\n");
    exit(0);
  }

  // Assign to structure members
  head->x                 = 5;
  head->y         = 34.78;
  head->next->x  = 6;
  head->next->y  = 45.89;
```

```
        // Display the values of linked structure members
        printf("head->x:  %d\n",head->x);
        printf("head->y: %f\n", head->y);
        printf("head->next->x:  %d\n",head->next->x);
        printf("head->next->y: %f\n", head->next->y);

        // Finished, deallocate memory
        free(head->next);
        free(head);

        return(0);
    }
```

Chapter 8

1. The **filecopy.c** program does what its name suggests, but uses
    command-line arguments to get the names of the files to copy.

```
        #include <stdio.h>
        #include <stdlib.h>

        void filecopy(FILE *, FILE *);

        int main(int argc, char *argv[])
        {
          FILE *inp, *outp;

          if (argc != 3)
          {
            printf("Program %s: Usage: %s <f1> <f2>", argv[0], argv[0]);
            exit(0);
          }
            if ((inp = fopen(argv[1], "r")) == NULL)
          {
            printf("Cannot open input file\n");
            exit(0);
          }
            if ((outp = fopen(argv[2], "w")) == NULL)
          {
            printf("Cannot open output file\n");
            exit(0);
          }
          filecopy(inp, outp);
          fclose(inp);
          fclose(outp);
          return(0);
        }
```

```
void filecopy(FILE *inp, FILE *outp)
{
    int c;
    while ((c = getc(inp)) != EOF)
        putc(c, outp);
}
```

2. Here's the version of **fsearch.c**, also done with command-line arguments:

```
#include <stdio.h>
#include <stdlib.h>
#include <string.h>

int strpos(char *, char *);
int main(int argc, char *argv[])
{
    char instr[100], *cp1, *cp2;
    int  matchct, pos, inlen;
    FILE *inp;
    if (argc != 3)
    {
        printf("Usage: %s <filename> <pattern>\n", argv[0]);
        exit(0);
    }
    if ((inp = fopen(argv[1], "r")) == NULL)
    {
        printf("Cannot open input file\n");
        exit(0);
    }
    matchct = 0;
    cp2 = argv[2];
    while ((fgets(instr, 100, inp)) != NULL)
    {
        // search each line until end file
        cp1 = instr;
        inlen = strlen(cp2);
        while ((pos=strpos(cp1, cp2)) >= 0)
        {
            matchct++;
            cp1 += (pos + inlen - 1);
        }
    }
    printf("%d occurrences of %s in file %s\n",
        matchct, argv[2], argv[1]);
    fclose(inp);
    return(0);
}
```

```c
int strpos(char *s1, char *s2)
{
    int    len;
    char    *lptr = s1;

    len  = strlen(s2);

    while (*lptr)
    {
        if ((strncmp(lptr, s2, len)) == 0)
            return(lptr - s1 + 1);
        lptr++;
    }
    return(-1);
}
```

3. Program **randio.c**:

```c
#include <stdio.h>
#include <stdlib.h>
#define NOT_OK 1
#define OK 0

struct file_rec
{
    char    fname[15];
    char    lname[15];
    int     age;
};

// Function prototype declarations

int f_create(void);
int f_display(long);
void disp_stdout(struct file_rec *);

int main(void)
{
    int c;
    int start_rec = 0;
    long start_off = 0;
    if ((f_create()) == NOT_OK)
    {
        printf("Couldn't create output file\n");
        exit(0);
    }

    fflush(stdin);
```

191

```c
      printf("\nThe file will now be displayed\n");
      printf("Print from the start? ");
      printf("Answer 'y' or 'n' and  RETURN: ");

      if ((c = getchar()) == 'n')
      {
         fflush(stdin);
         printf("Start with what record no.? \n");
         printf("Enter number and RETURN: ");
         scanf("%d", &start_rec);

         // Subtract one to get offset intended
         start_rec—;
         if (start_rec < 0)
            start_rec = 0;
         start_off = (long)start_rec * ((long)sizeof(struct file_rec));
      }

      if ((f_display(start_off)) == NOT_OK)
      {
         printf("Couldn't print file input\n");
         exit(0);
      }
      return(0);
}

int f_create(void)
{
   struct file_rec buf;
   FILE *outp;
   int c;

   // Create output file

   if ((outp = fopen ("file.dat", "wb")) == NULL)
   {
      printf("Couldn't open output file\n");
      return(NOT_OK);
   }

   do
   {
      // Enter one record of data
      printf("Enter first name, last name and age: ");
      scanf("%s %s %d", buf.fname, buf.lname, buf.age);

      // Get rid of any unwanted scanf stuff
      fflush(stdin);
```

```c
      // Write the record to the file
      if ((fwrite(&buf, sizeof(buf), 1, outp)) < 1)
      {
        printf("Can't write to output file\n");
        return(NOT_OK);
      }

      printf("Type RETURN to continue,'q' to quit: ");
    }
    while ((c = getchar()) != 'q');

    fclose(outp);
    return(OK);
}

int f_display(long start_off)
{
    struct file_rec buf;
    FILE *inp;
    int end_of_file = 0;

    if ((inp = fopen("file.dat", "rb")) == NULL)
    {
      printf("Can't open file input\n");
      return(NOT_OK);
    }

    if (start_off > 0)
      if ((fseek(inp, start_off, SEEK_SET)) != 0)
      {
          printf("Can't reach file offset\n");
          return(NOT_OK);
      }

    while (end_of_file == 0)
    {
      fread(&buf, sizeof(buf), 1, inp);
      if ((ferror(inp)) != 0)
      {
        printf("Error reading file\n");
        return(NOT_OK);
      }
      if ((feof(inp)) != 0)
      {
        printf("End of file reached\n");
        end_of_file = 1;
      }
      else
```

```
            disp_stdout(&buf);
        }
    fclose(inp);
    return(OK);
}

void disp_stdout(struct file_rec *buf)
{
    printf("\nName: %s %s\n", buf->fname, buf->lname);
    printf("Age: %d\n", buf->age);
}
```

Index

Symbols

#define 11
#include 11

A

Address arithmetic 121
Address-of operator 20, 66
Aggregate data types 18, 96
ANSI C 3
argc 126
Argument list 44
Arguments 15
argv 126
Arithmetic operators
  List of 30
Arrays 18
  assigning to pointers 37
  defining and initialising 86
  initialising multi-dimensional 88
  of pointers 124
  of structures 101
Arrow operator 104
Assignment 27
  to a structure 97
Assignment operator 62
Associativity
  of operations 65
auto storage class 52

B

Base address displacement calculation
    91
Boolean value 60
Branching 16
break statement 78
  compared to return 79

C

C preprocessor 11
C Standard Library 21

Call

Call
  by reference 48
  by value 48
  to function 9
calloc 117
Character
  array 89
  class tests 153
  constants 32
  pointer 14
  set 24
  zero 32
Comma operator 65
Command-line arguments 126
Compiler 5
Compound
  assignment 62
  condition 63
  statement 4, 8
Conditional
  operator, '?' 64
  statement 8
Constants 32
continue statement 78
Control flow 72
Conversionbetween data types 27
ctype.h 165

D

Data 7
Data types 18, 24
  programmer-defined 96
Declaration/definition, distinction 57
do-while loop 77
Dot operator 97
Dynamic storage allocation 117

E

else clause
  if statement 17, 74
EOF 15, 143
Equality operators 63

195